Searching...
for Normal: A
Memoir

By
Alison Neuman

Fireside Publications

To
Elizabeth
Best
Wishes
Alison
Neuman
!!

Fireside Publications II
5144 Harbour Drive
Oxford, Florida 34484

www.firesidepubs.com
Printed in the United States of America

This is a memoir of the author's life based in large part on medical records and verbal discussions between members of her family along with the oral history among her family and her medical team.

Names of persons, other than family members, have been changed to protect their privacy. Other names, characters, places and incidents are either the product of the author's memory/imagination or are used fictitiously.

First Edition: November 2013

For additional copies of *Searching for Normal, A Memoir* please visit:
   http://kadinbooks.com
   or contact the author at:
   aneuman@telusplanet.net

Dedication

With genuine love and affection, I'm
dedicating this memoir
To my loving family; my loyal friends; and to
my Heavenly Father.
With appreciation, for your strength
And guidance.

Acknowledgements

My appreciation and thanks for the role they played in the completion of this memoir go out to:

Lois Bennett – Fireside Publications
Jessica Henderson – Cover Consultant
Rachel Wood – My Gal-Friday Publicity

Kyla, Shelley, Jaclyn, Karen, Lynn, Rick, BD, Ian, Iris, Roxanne, Lindsay, Kelise, Julie, Alex, Stephanie, Curtis, Danielle, Dylan, Lola, Claire, Katherine, Chase, Liz, Rebecca, Isabelle, Marina, Justin, Angela, Belen, Stefina, Mickey, Sandra, Helen, Val, Babs, Wes, Jeff, Cheryl, Jeananne, Shawn, and Sherrill.

Athabasca University MAIS instructors and MacEwan General Studies and PROW instructors, support staff, and students. Capital Region physicians, surgeons, specialists, nurses, technicians, physical and occupational therapists, and hospitals.

Edmonton International Fringe Theatre Festival 2013, iDANCE Edmonton, CRIPSiE, and Orchesis Dance Group; And, anyone involved in the creation of books, music, radio, television, movies, or board and video games; You made the isolation vanish and inspired my imagination and creativity.

All the children who have had, and will have, to grow up too fast, and all the adults with the courage to let their inner child come out to play.

A Sense of Normalcy

Normal: "Conforming to a type, standard, or regular pattern."

The Merriam – Webster's Collegiate Dictionary (Tenth Edition)

My sense of 'normalcy' died when I was three and a half years old. What was first diagnosed as the flu soon mercilessly invaded my body and my life.

As I ached all over, became jaundiced and blood oozed from my pores, the doctors searched the world for anyone exhibiting the same symptoms. Of course, as this was in the 1970s, telephones and good old-fashioned time-consuming mail were the only options; this was more easily said than done. At one point, after spending thirteen weeks in various hospitals, my family was told to take me home – my case was terminal.

I have seen so many medical professionals throughout my life, it's difficult to keep track. And as a child, I got into the habit of assigning each one of them a nickname; I've identified them by using those nicknames throughout this book. Despite how I was treated by some of them, they all have played a part in ensuring my survival.

As a child the way the world viewed or categorized me was irrelevant. Perhaps it was because I was far too busy trying to reach and exceed the goals set by others, while fighting against a disease that took every opportunity to extinguish my normalcy – my dreams, my goals and ultimately, my life. My dad, mom and brother Cliff all worked to provide me with the most normal life possible. Despite various pains with my body randomly acting out of my control, and the frequency of doctors' appointments, it never even occurred to me that I was different – that I was not physically able, not intelligent enough, or not able to keep up with everyone else in the world.

But when I began attending school, I quickly came to the conclusion that in the eyes of my classmates, I was not normal. The recognition settled into my body, heart, and soul with a shock that was almost impossible to comprehend. I decided early on that I wanted to prove everyone wrong and never own that newly-imposed identity of difference.

This is my journey to reclaim my sense of 'normal' throughout my battle with dermatomyositis – an enemy that remained nameless to us for over a dozen years; and the stigma that attached itself to my life – a battle I continue to wage to this day.

Alison Neuman, February 2013

Chapter One

Summers were exciting when I was a child; I was able to play outside and explore the neighborhood in my family's and my best friend Tara's yard. Tara is two weeks younger than me and we lived just three houses apart from one another. She was active in sports, dancing and activities with her older siblings. During our visits, I was always struck by the massive size of her family's two-story house, which I was convinced was more like a castle, with its expansive space and numerous rooms. Having a larger house was essential for her family as Tara was just one of ten children

In their rumpus room were Fisher-Price toys, Barbie dolls, and a large variety of board games awaiting us – the sheer variety rivaled only by a toy store. Mom had quit her job as a nursing aide to stay at home and raise Cliff and me, and when the weather was warm enough, Tara and I would play in their large pie-shaped backyard while our Moms sat on the porch and chatted.

I remember sharing our excitement to attend Grade One. I had yet to perceive any difference between the two of us – sure, I had to attend doctors' appointments more often than she – but beyond that, I ran and played just like everyone else. That said, in the privacy of my home, I noticed a sequence of changes in my body that did not seem to be shared by my friends. And my six-year-old brain was incapable of understanding the reasons behind those changes.

Those first few years living with a mysterious illness, that no doctor seemed to be able to pin-point, were a blur; and I struggle to remember all of them with distinct clarity. What I was able to grasp from the medical jargon was that the stability of my health was no longer reliable.

I had calcifications traveling throughout my body, attempting to find an exit. When I was seated, finding a comfortable position was tough due to the little white calcifications that grew in pressure areas like my elbows and knees. The calcifications created pressure, and grew outward until the skin could no longer stand the strain; then they erupted in chunks of calcium-laced liquid and blood. Each time this occurred, my mom changed the bandages and kept an eye out for opportunistic infections.

As these changes progressed, I wanted to hide them from everyone. The impact of the all–too-frequent hospitalizations also started to take shape. Experience had taught me that hospitals were big impersonal buildings with nurses, doctors, strange aromas, and beds that trapped patients inside. I grew uncertain as to the permanence of my home life each time I was admitted. And courtesy of the evening news, I also began to think of hospitals and *homes* as a place where they sent the differently-abled when they had become too much of a burden to their families. These places looked like prisons, and I vowed to be as good as I could so that my family would not have a reason to send me away.

Until I had grown increasingly ill, to the point where the condition could no longer be ignored, my skin, muscles, and joints had gone unnoticed by me, and by the rest of the world. But now, I couldn't help being conscious of it all the time; my body was a constant cause of stress and unlimited distraction.

Each new calcification site played by its own rules; staying open and continuing to leak for weeks, months, and even years. Some calcifications would reopen while others would move around and choose new sites to target.

The joint pain was invisible, and so the strain, burning, and weakness in my muscles went unnoticed by many. Only scars seemed to be proof of a battle I had fought and won. Yet despite the victories, I longed for the smooth elbows of my family and friends. I wished I could have just a single spot to lean on without having to worry about bleeding.

I knew my health and body required frequent appointments to stay healthy, but when issues first started, they seemed endless. In order to begin tracking the progress of my disease, the doctors suggested a follow-up bone scan at the Cross Cancer Institute.

Tests were a blur of discomfort; I learned to block the experiences from my brain. This reliable and less invasive test began with an injection of radio-active tracer, then drinking water, and waiting. As I waited for the test to begin, my family set themselves up in what would soon become familiar positions – Mom doing word scrambles, Dad watching television in the lobby.

This room's sterility and mountain of foreign machinery was vaguely familiar. As the machine began its slow crawl the full length of my body, having to lay completely flat and still on the table became torturous. The calcifications began to burn, ache, and throb. Lying against the hard table, each one pinched the outer skin.

My mind fought my body's desire to bend and relieve the pressure – relief was just one muscle twitch away; intellectually I knew that by giving in and moving, the test would take longer, and require additional time to complete from where it left off. Eventually, the technician let Mom stay in the room, a safe distance from the scan area, to fill the test time with conversation and distraction.

After a few weeks, the scan's results showed that not only was the calcium traveling extensively, looking for new destinations to explore, but it had also decided to take up residence in my joints. My medical team explained it was similar to arthritis resulting in joint pain and difficult movement – it had also shrunken the actual size of my muscles, weakening them. The end result being that the more I fought my muscles, the more they would shake, surrender, and ultimately, fail me. When I fought to work the muscles, the condition responded by causing a burning sensation that no medication or rubbing could relieve.

Each time my mom had to change the bandages covering the calcifications, my skin was so sensitive that it left a red raw patch when it was removed. Each red, raw patch required healing time, so a new tape was needed. Bandage pads had a reputation for adhering to the sore and pulled off scabs with them. Relief was found only when Mom discovered paper tape and non-stick pads to use on my calcifications.

Even at seven, I understood the doctor's appointment had the potential for unpleasant surprises, or being very unpleasant and scary. Dr. Cowboy was of medium height and carried himself with a quiet, self-assured demeanour. Whenever he was unavailable to attend, he sent his associate, Dr. Pinches, a short chubby man with absolutely no sense of humor. On one particular visit, Dr. Cowboy discussed plans for my education.

School was the one thing I looked forward to, because I felt it would always be a haven, safe from the medical team's intervention. I knew every kid had to go to school, and my excitement had grown over the prospect of attending the school where Cliff had gone, and spending the classes with Tara.

So when Dr. Cowboy told Mom about a special school within the hospital that offered classes and therapy, I panicked, wondering if I had done something wrong. I saw Mom placate the doctor by taking his brochures, but placing them in her purse. I knew that every decision made in my life was made with both Mom and Dad involved, which was a comfort to me. And yet, it filled me with a sense of unease; I somehow knew my future was no longer as certain as it had once seemed.

But then came some good news. My doctors were following the case of another patient exhibiting similar symptoms. That other patient's body had stopped over producing calcium once the person became a teenager. They thought there was a good chance that would happen for me as well, and Mom and I shared a smile.

Despite Mom's urging, the medical team were reluctant to provide us with a name. One doctor even argued that it would do us no good to know the name anyway.

We weren't university-educated medical doctors, sure. But the fact remained that giving this disease a name would have empowered us all psychologically and emotionally.

The battle scars of my disease were starting to show all over my body, but I fought to keep moving and exploring the world. My family was also fighting to keep my life as normal as possible. Most of the time, I convinced myself that I was like everyone else, but memory of one summer evening lingers with me, in particular. Dad was going to take Mom and me out to Dairy Queen. I was proudly wearing one of my favorite summer dresses that fell just above my knees, and was ready to head over with them for some soft serve. Dad came over to Mom, scowled, and whispered something.

"Bill," Mom responded, "there's nothing wrong with her knees."

After both of them shared a look and a scowl, Mom helped me put on a pair of pants. The idea that my body and my scars made me ugly, lingered with me from that day forward. It made me keenly aware that people were going to look at my body and judge me, or even be repulsed by me. The concept of body image was now seared into my consciousness.

And then my parents had to make the difficult decision to send me to the special school, with the hope of giving me additional academic opportunities, while ensuring the best possible health care.

It devastated me, and reinforced my perception that being sent away was a sentence doled out to *different* people. Now my body was ugly, different, and shameful; and my one opportunity to feel normal had been stripped away. At my young age, I felt as though I had actively done something horrible that warranted having to leave my friends for the company of strangers.

Mom soon noticed that I was not as bubbly as usual, and had begun to isolate myself.

To me, it was a way of preparing myself for being alone.

But as she always had and always would, she broke through my isolation; with a hug, she reminded me how much they all loved me, and how I was a part of the family. I was not something they were ashamed of.

"Honey," she assured me, "I will never let anyone send you away."

The first day of Grade One began with sunlight creeping into my room. Dad had gone to work at the service station, but the house still had the aroma of bacon and eggs. This was my first day of traveling a path different from those of either my friends or my family. Dressed in my favorite new outfit, feeling semi-confident, I set out with Mom. My journey to classes began with a cab driving us to the school, which was housed in the hospital where I had clinic visits. This day we entered through the same large double doors as we usually did, only instead of going to the clinic area, we turned and walked down hallways that ended at an entrance where buses were unloading students.

I was struck by the similarities stuck to Tara's *regular* elementary school – the large black mat covering the entrance floor, the children's-height shelves full of boots and shoes of every color and size. All the decorations and child-sized benches were similar to the ones at the kindergarten I had been able to attend the previous year.

This school mirrored my elementary school, the only difference being that the students seemed to be exploring the world with various mobility aids. In the main office was a boy using a walker – his one leg seemed to catch, and it took him extra effort to move. A student raced by me in an electric wheelchair. As she sped by, her electric wheelchair hummed, and she smiled at me. I smiled back.

Having Mom with me made this new world seem less intimidating.

My teacher, Mrs. Bauer, provided me a written assessment test.

"We will assess her knowledge," she explained, "and see if she requires specialized assistance or has any learning deficits."

My head shook as I frowned, trying to grasp why they might think I had a learning deficit. My family was smart, I was smart! I had joint and muscle issues; but the assumption that mobility issues affected my intellect already stood out for me as a misperception on her part. How could my intelligence, or anyone's for that matter, be measured by my mobility, or the physical configuration of my body be relevant?

Yet there I was, forced to write the first of many tests. While I had no problem writing the same kind of tests my friends and family had in their school careers, I felt like this test was searching for my limitations, rather than assessing my level of knowledge.

Sure enough, the results indicated I had a Grade Two level in all my subjects except for math, allowing me to be in an advanced Grade One class. My knowledge, and all Mom's and my work helping me learn how to read and write was coming through.

The next challenge was certainly one shared by students in any school system – finding where I fit in. Being with adults was something familiar and comfortable to me, but being with other children of any age was not. While the two students at the special school seemed friendly, I was worried that I would not make friends. Then I remembered something Cliff had told me. On his first day of high school the football team asked him if he'd like to play, due only to his height. His height made him different, and he was embraced because of it. So I could make friends too.

On my second day of school a small yellow bus pulled up to our house and Mom escorted me down our sidewalk up to its steps. The school bus driver, Walter, made sure I had a front seat, next to Mike. Mike was skinny, pale and gave me very special gifts that day – that of friendship and a sense of belonging, as we traveled that literal and figurative journey together. Even though he was in a different classroom, we started and finished each day together. Even if all the students at the different school got around the world using aids to walk or wheelchairs, we were all going to school just like normal children.

Yet weekends visiting and playing with Tara reminded me how different our lives were. In school, she was having music classes with the classic *Statue Game*, a version of tag that involved freezing on spot; it was hard to imagine us playing such a game. Tara had gym. I had physiotherapy to improve and maintain my flexibility and occupational therapy, which focused on my hands and fingers. The therapy often drained my energy, and made focusing on the next class a challenge before my energy recharged.

Our recesses were similar in that both Tara and I played inside or outside at the playground. Even the special school had a courtyard surrounded on all four sides by the building.

Lunch times were very different though, with Tara walking home for lunch, while mine were spent in the cafeteria. But the cafeteria gave me the opportunity to meet others, and Mandy, a girl my age using a wheelchair with an aide to help her, became my good friend. We would eat lunch together, and race in the courtyard or gym together. If she required help getting her jacket on and off, or picking something up, I was always glad to help.

As I worked on improving my printing, I found holding a pencil challenging. My therapist put a rubber grip on my pencil to make it easier to hold, but pain and fatigue was a hindrance during printing practice. The only way to hold a pencil was to balance it between my thumb and my third finger. My second finger pointed up and out of the way – it had a mind of its own. Each time something like this came along, I began to notice the disparities between our experiences. My only consolation was that the next year the plan was for me to be back at my regular school, sharing the same subjects and activities with Tara.

Inevitably, my disease usually decided to stir things up just when I found I was about to relax and become comfortable in my circumstances. Dread filled me each time, knowing a doctor's appointment was approaching; and there was always a fear of being admitted to the hospital. Terror rattled in my small body like a winter breeze slapping me across the face.

Some months into the school year, a doctor's appointment once again led to me being hospitalized. There was a comfort having four other children in the room with me, but the time just emphasized to me that even having school in the hospital didn't guarantee me my health.

Down the hallway was a nursery. It was furnished with silver metal cribs and rocking chairs of rich, dark wood. From the window and door of my room, I could see into the nursery and enjoyed watching the parents with their children. The children were not all babies but were small enough to require a crib. Most of the parents would rock their children and calm them when they cried. Several children got better and could be seen smiling and leaving, hand in hand or in their parent's arms.

But one child never left the crib, and the parents rarely displayed joy on their faces. Even though I had been introduced to the concept of mortality with family members, I'd never thought about it in relation to children. There were teardrops falling down the woman's face, and the man pulled her close into his chest as they hugged. That evening, there was a rustle and alarms going off. Various staff rushed into the room bringing unfamiliar machines with them. When the alarms went silent, all the hospital room doors were closed, and several nurses and staff went into the smaller children's room. The following day, the crib was empty, the sheets stripped, mattress wiped, and the railings down just as they always are when a patient leaves.

11

I kept searching every day for her parents and expected her to be returned to her crib, to come back from a test or surgery, but she never did. The bed remained empty and another child moved in to receive care. My mind raced wondering if the child had gone to heaven, but it didn't seem possible – she was not *old*. As realization set in over the days, sadness filled my heart for the parents who would never get to see her talk, walk, and grow.

But more than being sad for her parents, I had my first realization that if those young children could die, I could die, also. Life and years were not guaranteed. The safety of knowing my family would always be with me was gone.

This awareness brought with it worry, and a sense of powerlessness every time I was separated from my family. It was a very real fear that would stay with me, and one not easily dealt with, even as an adult, let alone in childhood.

Chapter Two

My medical team continued to follow leads for the mystery of why my body was producing calcium and attacking itself. My life remained an unending wave of uncertainty, shuffling between being at home where there was a regular schedule and activities, to a variety of doctor visits and medical treatments. On this particular occasion, I'd been hospitalized after exposure to a neighbor who had contracted the measles; so I was kept in isolation.

Even at six, I understood the safety precaution to ensure no one became ill, but I really had no concept of what the measles were, or the complications they could elicit. As if coming to visit me and going through that wave of emotions was not already enough for my family, now it became much more of a procedure.

Outside my room, Mom and Dad got into yellow gowns, masks, and gloves. They looked like space movie astronauts with all their gear on. Even my room door was always kept closed; as they stepped in, the door made a suction sound similar to those from the *Star Trek* episodes I had come to know from the TV.

My days were punctuated by visits from the medical staff, but the only visits that brought me solace were from my mother. She usually came during the day and then traveled home to make supper for Dad. In the evening both Dad and Mom came to visit me. One night Dad came to visit me by himself, and I immediately wondered if my mother and Cliff's absence meant something was wrong. Dad seemed like the air had been knocked out of him. I had become used to sensing what people were feeling, beyond what they were saying – reading meaning from their body language. As a child I was used to being talked over, and I found this a useful survival technique to decipher all the mixed messages being sent out. I felt an energy, like a black cloud, around him. Dad explained that my grandfather was sick, and Mom was helping him. I was not to worry as Mom would be back to visit me tomorrow. I trusted Dad implicitly; he'd never given me a reason to feel otherwise.

That evening we sat, talked and watched *M*A*S*H* together. It was one of the most special evenings I shared with him as a young child. We sat and drew pictures including one of a woman's face with large lips. We called her "Hot Lips." Dad taped the picture to my hospital washroom door because it made us both laugh.

Too soon it was time for Dad to go home; he bent down and gave me a hug, as I told him to pass my wishes on to Mom and Cliff. When I asked him to tell Grandpa I loved him, I watched sadness creep into his eyes; but when he hugged me and stood up, his face was bright again.

I learned later that my Grandpa had died from a massive heart attack. Everyone was strong, and other than a few teary eyes now and again, the grieving process went on without my noticing a great deal. I knew Grandpa was old and had gone to heaven, but his absence didn't affect me that much, until after my release.

Life went on as usual until a few days later, when we went to visit Grandma K and my Uncle Ingmar. Grandpa K was not there – not sitting in any of the rooms or watching television. I realized that I had to adjust to the reality that there would be no more going with Grandpa K to the corner store and buying a Revel for all of us; no more hugs cloaked with the smells of cigars and peppermints. Our lives would always have an empty spot reserved just for Grandpa K, only.

Back at school my life continued as before, with the regular series of classes and homework and therapy. My least favorite subject was math; I found that having to concentrate and figure out how to complete the questions was challenging for my medicated and tired brain. When my body ached, and I had trouble getting comfortable, being able to focus on anything was a challenge in itself. The more issues I had with grasping math, the less confidence I had in myself. I started to wonder if I might not be as bright as others. My struggle with math began in earnest from that point forward.

The physiotherapy was broken down into daily sets of range of motion movements, to reduce stiffness and keep my joints flexible. The exercises were actually enjoyable, although I would not admit this to any therapists since doing so would invite extra repetitions. Each exercise worked my head, arms, legs, trunk, fingers, and feet. Stretching exercises used more energy, forcing me to reach further and improve my flexibility. The more painful exercises required the use of large thick rubber bands, in different colors denoting their level of resistance, which I pulled to build my muscles. Isometric exercises kept the joints static while

I worked the muscles. Then I ended with isotonic exercises, which worked both the muscles and the joints together.

The stretches and isotonic exercise always caused my body to ache and my energy level to drop. But, a powerful serge went through me knowing that I was, in some small way, taking back control from a body that was raging a war against me; and that was a victory for my spirit.

Tara had gym and sports to improve her general skills and ability. I had therapy with exercises to keep my body from surrendering to the progression of my disease as it stole my independence and mobility.

I could never really escape the fear that the disease would find a new vulnerability in my body. Sitting at a listening station during music class, my neck started to ache and burn; and my heart sank. I'd had these episodes at home, but they had gone unnoticed by the medical team. Previous experience had taught me that new attacks lead to more painful examinations and a potential hospitalization; I knew my neck would draw unwanted attention.

In a desperate attempt to hide the truth, I leaned my head on my arm and acted as if everything was fine. Mrs Bauer was preoccupied with something at her desk. My head fell to the side, and the muscles were not strong enough to support my now heavy head.

Not again. Not here.

After one last unsuccessful attempt, my head surrendered, and fell down towards my shoulder. The headphones that a few minutes ago felt only mildly heavy, now felt like one of the ten-pound bags of potatoes Mom brought home from the grocery store.

By now, Mrs. Bauer was kneeling down and watching me. Despite trying to convince her that my neck episode would resolve itself in time, she argued with me, citing her responsibility to keep me safe. She made a call at her desk while I took a deep breath, trying to summon up my courage.

I would have swallowed deeply as well, but every time I tried, it felt like my throat was two sizes smaller than it was.

Of course I was required, with my physiotherapist in tow, to be examined by yet another doctor. He was younger, and he talked to me as he moved and examined my neck. After the exam and an X-ray, I went back to class and attempted to resume my day.

The pain was distracting, and it was a challenge to hold my head up. I held my arm under my head to provide support but it offered little comfort. Once my mother arrived, we returned to the doctor's office where they discussed the best course of action to aid my weak muscles: physio, medication, and a neck brace.

The neck brace was uncomfortable and made swallowing a bit of a challenge; but my head sat straight with it, which reminded my muscles how they were supposed to behave. There was no way to hide the brace and I felt like it flashed a neon sign at my physical difference, but the doctor assured us that with his recommendations, my neck would get better.

We walked back up to my classroom to get my stuff. Classes were over, and the hallways were empty. Teachers were setting the chairs up on the tables.

Mrs. Bauer and Mom began discussing a puppet show the class was going to have, and she extended an offer for me to be the narrator. She was under the impression that I would be a natural with people. I eagerly agreed.

My neck improved as the weeks leading up to the puppet show passed. My family was coming to watch, and I was excited since Tara was also going to be in a play at her school; we were finally able to share in the excitement of similar activities, despite our different schools.

Finally the day of our production of the "*Three Billy Goats Gruff*" arrived. There was an air of excitement highlighted by the aroma of construction paper and glue as we handcrafted our puppets. No matter how hard I tried, one side of my goat was backwards; so no matter how I held it, the thing always walked backwards.

"It gives the goat personality," Mrs. Bauer said. "And as they say in show business, 'the show must go on,' backwards gait or not!"

Our classroom was transformed with seating and a puppet show tower. We hid behind the tower, and got our puppets ready.

There were no expectations in my mind as to what was going to happen or how having a backwards puppet would come off to the audience. When my puppet popped up in the cut-out, I tried desperately to make him walk forward, but he always wound up heading the other way, and I found myself smiling. From behind the large cardboard stage, the audience was laughing – and the sound was wonderful. The laugher was for my puppet – *not my disease, not at me* – it was *for* me. And at that point, it was done – the stage bug had bitten me. That love of limelight would stick with me forever.

At home, Cliff had hit a milestone that I dreamed of every day. He was soon posing in his graduation cap and gown, while Mom captured the moment on camera. He pulled me over to join him in front of the long living room curtains, and we both gave our best *photo* smiles. Then Cliff took off his grad cap and placed it on my tiny head. The tassel tickled my face, and once they looked at me, they both started laughing. We laughed so hard that my face turned red.

Click.

Mom took a snapshot of a moment of joy that my disease couldn't steal away from us.

I remember that day from that moment; and from when Cliff made a point of saying that I'd wear my own cap and gown, and it would fit me just right. His confidence in my ability made me feel like getting a high school diploma was truly an achievable goal

As the school year came to a close, I made sure to enjoy spending the last few bus rides with Mike. While I would miss talking with him, there was an entire summer ahead of me. We both had lives and friends beyond that bus, and the end of this year meant that we would both be able to resume those lives full-time. As I stepped off the bus on the last day, my heart skipped a beat. I was going to miss them – Mandy, Mike. Walter, and maybe even my therapists, but this was home. No *special* bus trips to a *special* school with *special* activities.

But as much as I'd been loath to attending a *special* school, we students had all developed a weird kinship because of how different our lives were from the rest of the world. It gave us all an immediate bond that only *we* shared. Along those lines, Dr. Cowboy suggested I attend a special summer camp. *Special* meaning it was designed for children who are differently-abled or challenged. The duration of the camp was only a few days, and it was not too far away from the city. My friends had all gone to day camps before, but they'd never spent the night. And while I wanted to go to camp like them – or more accurately, *with* them – I wasn't too sure about spending the nights away from my family. Nightmares chased my sleep as the thought of awakening in a strange place, surrounded by strange people, began to seem less like *fun*, and a lot more like *risk*.

Chapter Three

As is usual in summer, the days went by quickly. While awake, I tried to absorb all the sounds and smells from home, since soon I was going to be away at camp. It was an adventure I had chosen to go on, but the fear that I might never see my family again always traveled with me wherever I would go. As the warm morning sun peeked through a crack in the curtains, I climbed out from the warmth and security of my bed. My clothes were waiting for me at the end of the bed. My heart skipped with a beat of excitement realizing *this was the day.*

Our home was a hive of activity, and an aroma drifted into my room – bacon and eggs that stirred my hunger. In the main room, the table was set, and my family was laughing and talking. While we all chatted freely about our lives, secretly I was having doubts about attending camp. I hid my fear from them, because in my mind, big girls were not scared. I hadn't yet grown to understand that even adults get scared sometimes.

As we pulled up to the bus area, I saw many other children walking or using walkers and wheelchairs for mobility. While I was gladdened to see them here, more than anything, I wanted my neighborhood friends to attend with me. I wanted a camp where children with and without special needs were all together and having fun, rather than having to leave our friends and family behind.

Dad carried my suitcase and special sleeping bag to the bus where our luggage was loaded into the bottom compartment. In our family, every goodbye always included an "I love you" and a hug; but when Mom and I embraced, I didn't want to let go. I forced myself to release my arms; and Dad's cologne clung to me as I joined a line of children waiting to enter and find their seats on the bus. Most of the other children talked loudly and bounced around in their seats. I tried so desperately to be carefree, but fear remained an unwanted companion.

The camp was fifty miles from the city, but to me it might as well have been across an ocean. I could reach my family by telephone, but unlike when I was in hospital, they wouldn't be able to just hop into the car and reach me in a few minutes. Along the drive, the shape of the landscape morphed from typical city buildings, traffic, and paved roads, to miles and miles of gravel, dirt roads, and trees.

Once the bus arrived at the camp, all the excited campers gathered in the middle of a quiet, grassy area. I joined them, trying to live in the moment, and just enjoy being there.

As we explored the camp, a twinge of sadness crept into my thoughts when I remembered I was worlds away from my family and friends. Welcoming each camper was a warm quilt resting on her bed. Our guide directed us to have a look around and make ourselves comfortable.

A group of girls, myself included, fanned out to explore all the cabin rooms. Relief washed over me when I discovered we had the luxury of an indoor toilet and tub. Due to my limited mobility and strength, my bed was not one of the bunk beds that the other campers were enjoying climbing up on.

Tara slept on a bunk bed at her house, but I never could join her, if she climbed up to the top bunk. This would be the same.

There were other campers with health challenges. One girl had to have the medical staff intermittently pound and rub her back and chest daily; another girl had no use of her body from the neck down; and the girl in the bed next to me was incredibly tiny and small for someone her age.

Daily activities provided me with the necessary distractions to keep my mind busy and interrupt any focus on pain or my family back at home. But at night, tucked into my bed, I lay in the darkness and stillness.

Alone.

It was even quieter than a hospital, and silent tears ran down my cheeks. The bravery I had fought so hard to display melted away as exhaustion set in. My pillow became damp.

Seeing this, Laura, our cabin's younger counsellor, sat next to me and suggested calling my Mom. With my shoes on, we walked across the grassy area to the main building. Once inside, Laura led me over to the telephone, and I dialed home. It rang three times. And with each ring the fear crossed my mind that something had happened, and I'd be left alone in this big, scary world.

As Mom's sweet voice said "Hello," it washed away my insecurities. Mom told me about their day, and I told her about mine. With the kind of reassurance only a mother can give, and our '*I love yous*,' we said our goodbyes. As we walked back to the cabin, the dark velvet sky was illuminated by the stars, and the large moon gave me hope that camp would be as much fun as the camp Tara was attending.

As I awoke, my face was warmed by sunlight peeking through the window. The air was fresh and carried the scent of spruce trees and an excitement about what activities the day would bring. Countless different birds chirped their own special songs. Inside the main cabin, everyone was trying to talk at the same time. We ate breakfast amid the aroma of bacon and cinnamon before walking over to the pier.

A flat boat ramp enabled wheelchairs and walkers to get up onto the boat deck from the dock. Shane, a 'rock star' styled counsellor with spiked hair was waiting for us on the boat. After a quick safety lesson, and once all of us had our life jackets on correctly, the boat slowly pulled away from the dock. The boat engine was humming, a gentle breeze was blowing across the water, and in that moment, the doctors were miles from here. I was miles away from the poking, the prodding and the procedures. I felt at peace.

The boat slowed before coming to a stop, the waves lapping against the side of the boat. We were each shown how to use a fishing rod. Shane showed us how to take a worm and put it on the hook; then Laura showed us how to toss the line in the water. Her line landed a fair distance from the boat, while my line fell directly into the water, close to the boat. Then, we waited; and waited; and waited for a fish to bite the poor dead worm. We waited for something to pull on the line so we could pull it in and be proud of our catch. We waited in vain.

The next morning as I prepared for the day, my stomach began to feel uncomfortable. It felt just like when I'd had the flu – I felt like I wanted to throw up. After morning chores, I climbed back on my bed to try to get my stomach to calm down, but my efforts were for naught. Despite my best efforts to race to the washroom, I threw up on the cabin floor. Embarrassment and disappointment filled me, as I continued on to the washroom.

Life to this point had taught me that when I made plans, my life and health made sure to stop them, but knowing that made the situation no less of an emotional blow. Tonight was the night we were scheduled to sleep outdoors in a tent. The main reason I had come to camp was to sleep in a tent, and we had bought a new sleeping bag just for that.

My disappointment was compounded by the fact that being at camp meant I no longer had the safety and security of my mom being there when things took a turn for the worse. While I was certain that being this far away from town meant it would be a *doctor-free-zone*, I was mistaken. Apparently there was a doctor who paid regular visits to the camp, and one was quickly summoned for me.

I used all my skills of negotiation, and made a bargain with the counselors and doctor that if I was no longer sick by the time we were going to sleep in the tents, I still could go. Until then, my spaghetti-like feeble legs carried me back to bed where I would sleep the day away. The aches and nausea did not disturb my sleep, and the only movements I made were to drink water and visit the washroom. Campers came in and out during their daily activities, and before I knew it, I

25

woke to a cabin filled with campers packing for the trip.

Laura was standing in the corner helping another camper with her bag, as I slowly sat up and dangled my feet off the edge of the bed. For a moment my head felt a bit woozy, but soon it cleared. To test my recovery, I walked to the bathroom and washed my face before returning to my bed. Success – I was going to be allowed to sleep in the tent.

While I didn't feel a hundred percent better, my stomach was holding its own. My body was blanketed with aches and weighed down by exhaustion, but I kept that my secret. When it was time to leave, I got up and went over to where my sleeping bag was waiting. Laura grabbed my sleeping bag, and we walked behind the cabins and down a path of worn-down grass. The fresh air brushed against my face, and I found myself smiling and laughing. By now, my legs were wobbly, but I kept the tent peak off in the distance as the motivation to push on.

The sun was setting beneath the trees, painting the sky with orange and pink hues. When we arrived at the tent, the counselors set the sleeping bags in rows so we could nestle in like peas in a pod. When the sun had set, the bright white moon and stars provided us with natural nightlight. Reserving all my energy from the day for the walk over to the tent was absolutely worth it.

We all got inside and snuggled down in the cool night air. My heart beat quickly with the excitement of the adventure – and excited too that my body hadn't spoiled my plans after all. Snuggled beneath my sleeping bag, I was warm and cosy with the knowledge I had achieved another victory. I closed my eyes and listened to the birds chirping and the peaceful silence. Sleep came immediately and lasted until morning. In the brisk morning air, we walked back to camp and our cabins. It seemed a much shorter walk than the night before.

The idea of being submerged under water was not something that had ever appealed to me. My family and medical team had made a point of explaining my body's lack of strength; as a result, I'd never even entertained swimming as an activity. But yet there I was in my swimsuit, wrapped in my towel, the warm summer air caressing my pale legs and my scars. Despite my best efforts to cover all my scars, there just wasn't enough towel. We walked along a worn dirt path, through the grass and lumpy dirt. Soon, the large, intimidating river came into view. As we got closer, the sound of the current grew louder and louder. I was less than sure about going into a river that made such a furious noise.

At the edge of the water several of us waded in, while our counselors stood and watched within reach. The water lapped up at my feet, and tempted me to go deeper. With every small step the water slapped against my legs threatening to unearth me. My legs were not sturdy; and not possessing any swimming ability, kept me from continuing into the strong water.

A short way down the river, there was a large brown protruding rock that at least two adults could sit on comfortably. Most of my fellow campers, with a counselor escort, were walking over to the rock. The kids sat on the rock in view of an amazing waterfall. I cautiously waded into the cool water towards the rock; my curiosity was getting the better of me. With each step, I fought the current and tried to ensure my footing was secure. It took me twice as long as everyone else to approach the rock.

Before I reached the rock and the safety of sitting down and resting my legs, a boy came up behind me and gave me a rough push. I fought to keep my balance, to avoid slipping into a river that would swallow me up and carry me away. But he pushed me again, this time even more roughly, with his full body weight.

A mix of anger and fear rose in my chest. My body would not be strong enough to hold on forever. As he lined up to give me one last good shove, I yelled at him to stop. The boy turned and scowled; and before I knew it, Laura was next to me in the water. She helped me over to the rock where I could enjoy the view. There I sat on the rock for some time, and watched the water rush down the horizon and disappear down the waterfall. But the whole situation had done little to quell my anxieties about water.

The next morning, I was greeted with the fact that it was my last day of camp. In a few short hours I would be on my way to my family, my home, and my friends; and I couldn't wait.

I left knowing that the camp had been an opportunity I'd filled with success. I had overcome my fears and even a brief battle with my health, and for a short while, I felt *able*. I felt independent.

The following Monday, Mom began the quest to try and find out if I could attend Grade Two at the regular school with Tara. The main problems lay in the label of *special need* that had been attached to me –

and even then it carried with it connotations of a disability. The mobility issues, caused by the arthritis in my joints, made me unable to participate in a *regular* gym class and run around with the other children. My mother was told bluntly that the school did not have the time to have a teacher help me on and off with my shoes. At home, getting help with everyday activities was never a problem.

Simple tasks like slipping on and off my sneakers, and sliding my jacket over my stiff and sore arms, were done without a second thought. Already, the world was sending me a message that, because I needed help with something they perceived of as *simple*, I was really not wanted. But they acquiesced, instead telling her that a student would be able to help me.

On the first day of Grade Two, Mom and I walked out of the house and towards the elementary school. My body was pumping with energy. Mom was going to volunteer some days in the library so she would be there for me, which eased some of the stress of going to an entirely new place with new people. Thanks to the help of other students, I settled into a rhythm faster than I'd expected; and I began to feel a growing sense of independence. In fact, I began to feel so confident that I started to push my boundaries.

The school was a ten-minute walk from our house, and I attended along with Tara. Her sister, Maria, went to the junior high close by, so we walked together each day. On one particular day, the girls reminded me they had an extra-curricular activity and would be late walking home, so I'd have to wait until they were done before leaving the school grounds.

After the last bell rang, I sat on a bench and watched the students all leaving the building. First students and parents gathering their items headed out for the day; next the teachers and some of the office staff left. Then the hallway was quiet, and only an occasional student walked by. The big clock in the hallway ticked loudly by each second. The hands taunted me as they traveled slowly across the face. I wanted to go home; so I began to trace the route home in my mind. Confident that I would have no problem making it home safely, I grabbed my bag and headed towards the exit.

First obstacle – the large heavy school doors. Using my body as leverage, I shoved it open to give me access to the tarmac and grass. Just as I had done every day walking home with the girls, I followed the path that had worn through the once lush grass, until I reached the sidewalk. After traveling the same way every weekday, twice a day, I was positive I could find my way home.

There was no traffic as I crossed the street and walked away from the shoebox-shaped bungalows and towards the familiar house with the large rock resting on the lawn. I rounded the corner to our crescent poles circling my neighbor's hedges acting as a signpost that home was just a few steps away.

My heart filled with pride, but pride that soon turned to guilt when Mom explained that the fact that I hadn't told Maria and Tara of my plans was a major problem. She told me they were likely frantic wondering where I was; and she promptly called both the school, and Tara's Mom, to let them know I was safe.

I felt a pit in the bottom of my stomach at the trouble I'd caused. But yet, deep down, I still felt proud of what I'd done in the larger scheme of things. Even though I continued to enjoy the company of my friends on walks to and from school, the fact that I had given myself the option of completing this task on my own signified something much greater. It gave me a level of independence – some form of normalcy. That was something I never again took for granted.

One of the rites of passage for most of the little girls in my neighborhood was becoming a member of the Brownies. Since our neighbor was the local troop leader, and Tara was a member, Mom let me join them as an extra-curricular activity. Once a week after school we met to learn about camping, cooking, crafts, sewing and singing; then we spent our breaks racing around the gym.

One particular week, the troop began planning a camping trip where they'd be earning related badges. When I'd joined the Brownies, I accepted I would be unable to get the physical activity badges, but that was not going to stop me from achieving as many other badges as my health would permit. But the feelings of isolation coming from not being included, then later hearing all about their achievements was difficult. Only *normal* children went to *normal* camp. This was another way society was telling me that *normal* was not a group I belonged to.

As we were about to join the troop huddle, I pulled a chair over. One of the grey-haired leaders sauntered over and insisted I get down on the floor, and sit with my troop.

I sat there for a moment in absolute shock. My medical team had given Mom instructions which she conveyed to the leaders about the importance of minimizing the opportunity for injury or pain. One of the things I was to avoid was getting down on the floor where the pressure could create a potential area for the calcifications to target. I looked up at the leader, and down at the hard gym floor. Despite my protestations, she would not hear of it, and began pointing at the floor, towering over me and ordering me to get off the chair.

I promptly stood up, carried my chair back over to the corner of the room, exited the gym, and continued on out of the school. I was just about to enter the playground when Tara reached me, and talked me into coming back. We walked back to the tarmac where another Brownie was holding open the doors for me.

Not another word was said about my sitting on the floor, but the damage had been done. Once inside, my troop took turns playing the *static game* where we all ran around the gym in our socks collecting static, and then shocking someone.

Even that game left me feeling isolated as I was on the receiving end of most of the shocks, since running and scraping my feet was so uncomfortable. The brownies all talked about their assignments and extra-curricular dance or sport activities; their lives were so very full and busy. The inclusiveness I had hoped for from the Brownies, yet again, failed to materialize.

Chapter Four

For most children, recess is the highpoint of their day. The rest of the school day is just something to get through between recesses. But as usual, my health issues had also asserted themselves into my playtime. Even if someone just casually bumped into me, pain would wrack my body. Those impact points then became potential spots for the calcium to collect and escape.

Between the immediate pain, and the possibility of ending up with more sores, I dreaded going outside with the other students. While here, too, there was an agreement between my medical team, my mom, and the school administration about allowing me to stay inside for recess; there was one teacher who would routinely ignore the policy. But just as it was with the Brownies, a six year old is powerless against an adult bent on ignoring medical advice – powerless.

On one occasion in particular, this teacher was confident the fresh air would be good for me, and insisted I go out. Despite my best efforts trying to explain why I had to stay inside, in her mind I was only a small child, and could not possibly know what was best for my body. Mom was not volunteering that day, so I had no recourse; I was on my own.

I slowly walked out onto the tarmac and sat on the side, out of the way of all the racing and laughing children. I had become used to watching from the sidelines, but I still longed to be with the students playing on the monkey bars and having a game of kickball. A classmate approached me and asked me to race her. There's something about racing when you're a child, that's just irresistible, and with the teacher's voice in my head telling me that it would be good for me, I gave in, thinking *what harm could come from participating in just one normal activity.*

"Ready. Set. Go!" she yelled. We both took off running. My heart was racing. My body was jolted every time my feet landed on the hard concrete. The breeze blew through my hair and for just one moment, I felt free – the same kind of freedom you get when you hit the peak of height on the swings. I turned my head to see where the girl was, and she was a distance behind me, and then ... my foot stuck on something on the tarmac.

I lost my balance and gravity took hold. My weak fingers and hands reached out to brace myself against the fast-approaching ground, knowing that they would soon make contact. First my knees cracked onto the uneven rocky tarmac; then my elbows slammed into the ground gave under the weight of my body. My body did little to cushion the speed of my impact; and next my forehead slammed into the tarmac – the sound of the contact echoing in my head. Pain shot like a bolt throughout my body. For a moment, I just lay there looking at the sewer cover a short distance from my body, its smells wafting nearby.

My classmate rushed over to see if I was okay. I slowly began to turn myself over onto my back, and she helped pull me onto my feet. I stood there for a minute, my arms and legs shaking. My forehead was wet; my hands were scratched and dusty. Instinctively, I wiped my hand across my forehead and as I brought it back down, I saw it was covered in blood. My pant legs were also soaked through with blood around my knees.

My friend had run over to the supervisor, alerting her to what had happened.

The matronly woman took one disgusted look at me.

"Go back in the school and wash yourself off," she said. Once you're cleaned up, return here. You'll be fine."

I passed through the empty hallways to the bathroom. With my foot on the water pedal, I washed my hands at the sink, and looked into the mirror. My smooth forehead was covered with scratches, blood, and dirt. My hands shook as I sat down and rolled up my pant legs in an effort to wipe off my knees. The pants would have to be washed at home; the last thing I needed was wet pant legs. My elbows were bruised and scratched, but fortunately not bleeding.

What was I thinking? I wasn't like the other children. And I knew it!

I walked back outside and returned to sitting on the high curb, watching the other children running around having fun. My knees had already started to stiffen; it quickly became a challenge just to get them to bend. Soon the bell rang and with effort, I pulled myself up off of the curb and slowly walked back into the school.

Back at the safety of my desk I tried to get my arms to stop shaking. My teacher could sense something was off, and once the class was settled, she walked over to my desk and looked at me. She promptly escorted me to the nurse's office, scolding the lunch supervisor for not sending me to the nurse sooner. We walked slowly down the hallway and into the nurse's office. The nurse had me lie down on the bed while she called my mother.

By now my forehead had stopped bleeding, but it throbbed. As I ran my hand along my forehead in an effort to relieve the throbbing, I felt a tender lump protruding from the spot where I had struck the pavement.

The nurse announced stiffly that my mom would be there soon to take me home. She walked over to me and put an ice pack on my forehead.

I lay quietly on the cot, covered in crisp white sheets.

Mom soon poked her head in the room and walked over to me. She wasn't angry at me for attempting to run and play like other children. But she certainly did not hold back with the teacher who had ignored the advice of a team of medical experts, and whose actions served to leave me nauseated and recovering from a concussion for several days.

I spent my seventh birthday in hospital. While Dr. Sunshine presented me with a humongous chocolate chip cookie, the day felt very much like any other day, with a round of tests and appointments, and some poking and prodding. I understood that my health was more important than a birthday party, but it's still difficult for a child to get past the sadness of not having the usual celebration. My disease had done it again – it had stolen another important milestone from me.

As the day wore on, I felt a real sadness creep in. I brightened only when my family appeared in the evening with a large Black Forest cake.

All the patients and staff came into the lunchroom, sat along the tables, and shared the cake. The elements of a birthday celebration materialized around me. Patients ran around. Patients laughed. Even bed-ridden patients smiled. Nurses relaxed, and for a brief amount of time there was only happiness. No uncertainty. No painful procedures. No loneliness. I forgot we were in a hospital. My family was here, and I was surrounded with love. I was able to appreciate how lucky I was to share this event with some other children and their families, who were also on a journey of *difference*.

Soon after my birthday, I was released and returned home to join my life again.

On my way to school one day, I was walking past the junior high when two boys who attended my school came up behind me. One of them crowded next to me trying to block access to the street, and then shoving me hard against the green metal fence. His friend laughed at me from the sidelines before joining in himself.

Tears threatened to fill my eyes, but I would not give them the satisfaction. Knowing that if I fell I would be stranded on the ground, I channeled all my focus to balancing and transferring my weight, ensuring that each step I took could withstand the blows. The boys' laughing echoed in my ears. I stopped. Then I stepped away from the fence and put my hands on my hips, in defiance.

"Don't do that!"

"Don't do that," the boy said in a high-pitched voice intended to mock me.

With angry determination, I started walking, and once again the boys took turns shoving me. I was prepared, and stood strong against each push. The school was only a few steps ahead, and I was determined that no matter what, I would endure.

This was about more than just the two bullies blocking my path to the school. It was about taking control. Those boys had no idea, but rather than instilling weakness or a sense of fear in me, their actions gave me strength and confidence, and helped me to find my own voice.

As the school year progressed, my struggles with math continued to frustrate me. I frequently stayed after school where my teacher, Mrs. M., would help me try and make sense of the jumble of numbers before me. Each time I wrapped my head around a concept, I was confident that the next assignment would be easier. But I still found each subsequent assignment was still a challenge. Deep in my subconscious an attitude that my struggles were related to my illness began to form. I couldn't help but think back to all the comments I'd encountered along the way that made me feel as though my mobility issues really did mean I would never be smart enough.

As the end of the school year approached, pride filled me to know I had almost completed a full year of classes, and held my own academically. But then one day Mrs. M insisted I stay after class for a meeting with my mother; I knew something wasn't right. Mrs. M discussed my achievements, and how I had excelled in all subjects, except for the dreaded math.

Then she uttered a phrase that I did not see coming.

"Alison," she said, "will have to repeat Grade Two."

I felt a pit form in my stomach, and tears of frustration gathered in my eyes.

All the long days staying after school to work on the math exercises; all the evenings spent working on the assignments; all the tutoring; all my work and efforts had been for nothing. The teacher had no faith in my ability, and was certain there just wasn't enough time for me to catch up to the Grade Three students. To her, I was stupid.

I watched Mom and Mrs. M exchange glances – Mom's of disappointment, and Mrs. M.'s of remorse. My mind raced to figure out why the other students' efforts paid off, but mine didn't. Was I really dumb?

Tara and I had finally been able to share the same classes together. Now she was moving on, and I was not. Despite all my best efforts, and having excelled in every other subject, I was going to be held back. My best was not good enough. My smart was not smart enough.

We walked home in silence, my disappointment written all over my face.

"Honey, teachers can be funny," Mom said. "When I was younger than you, my mom taught me my alphabet, math, and how to read. With all my knowledge, I showed up for the first day of Grade Two. But back then all the grades were in one small school house, and the teacher held me back in Grade One."

"Were you disappointed?"

"Absolutely, but it didn't stop me from finishing my education and continuing on to be a nursing aide." Mom smiled and stood up tall.

While Mom's story did exactly what a mother's words of encouragement should, I couldn't shake the feelings of frustration. Just shy of eight years old, I still had a feeling of being in a race against time, and being held back just served to create a greater urgency in me.

Chapter Five

My ankle was the next target for calcification. It snuck up on me until one day upon examination, I noticed a raised lump protruding out of the skin about an inch and a half from my left ankle. The skin was a reddish-purple color; the lump was pliable and filled with a white liquid substance. Pulling a sock or shoe over the lump was a painful impossibility. Any pressure caused the constant throbbing to grow even more intense. The more it grew, the more it throbbed, and the greater the inevitability of another trip to the hospital. Just allowing my foot to hang caused an immense swell of pressure in the area, and sent a burning pain rushing towards my foot; we had no choice but to make a trip to see Dr. Sunshine.

At the hospital, Dr. Sunshine slowly slid off my sock and gently examined the lump. Even the feel of his breath on my ankle caused me to inhale sharply. A puzzled look crossed his face. He leaned back in complete expectation that we were unlikely to be happy with what he was about to say; a hospital wristband soon signaled the beginning of a new incarceration.

The view from my hospital window this time was of the courtyard and its surrounding. I was at least able to observe some of the life below. Sleep escaped me for much of that night; I could never relax when I didn't know what might happen next. Too soon, the

41

nurse came in with a wheelchair and pushed me into a sterile room with green tiles lining the floor and walls. Mom accompanied me, grilling the nurse on whether this was a test that was absolutely necessary. But it appeared that it was, and the nurse lifted me up onto a stretcher and took off my sock.

The room reeked of cleaning antiseptic that made my nose burn; and the coldness of the room caused the lump on my foot to throb even harder. I did not like this room; it looked like a torture chamber, with its sterile cabinets and the shiny metal instruments, the gauze and bandages. Before long, a new doctor came in the room and examined the lump. My eyes stung from the inspections, but I refused to allow any tears to escape. Mom rubbed my arm, reassured me, and gave me strength to hang on.

He rubbed the lump with a cold alcohol pad then walked over to a counter in the corner of the room and returned with a large needle in his hand. Without any warning at all the needle was plunged into my skin in order to freeze the lump. While I knew the purpose of the injection was to numb the area where they'd be drawing a sample from, it had hurt more than I expected.

Mom wiped away the tears I could no longer hold back as we waited for the freezing to take effect; I was angry that I couldn't handle the freezing like a big girl. Mom tried to distract me, talking about going outside and Dad coming to visit. But all I wanted was for the medical staff to leave, for the world to pause so I could get a grasp on what was going on and regain some control. I wanted for once to be able to have a say, to have the ability to tell the doctors *NO* – to be a person, not a disease, not invisible.

Soon the doctor returned and poked an even larger needle into the lump. It felt like an electrical current was running through me as the needle drew out bloody yellow liquid. The pain afterwards was intense, and I was given painkillers to keep it under control. The lump throbbed and burned but gradually the pain lessened.

Mom helped me with my coat and transferred me into the wheelchair, covering me up with a thick warm blanket so that we could wander outside for a while. By the time we reached the elevator, I knew freedom was near.

The familiar hospital aromas that were so prevalent upstairs were mercifully mild in the main hospital lobby. In the distance, beyond the doors, was a world of freedom.

The sliding glass doors opened and a light breeze caressed my face, as we walked down the paved pathway to enjoy a bite of the cool, fresh air. The time when I had to return to the confines of the ward always came much too soon.

I awoke the next morning full of promise and hope. I'd had a good night's sleep, and for a moment or two I even forgot where I was. My room was covered in brilliantly-colored murals of an orange giraffe, a grey elephant, and a yellow lion; and the colors shone brightly in the sun. The door opened and yet another doctor entered to announce they were going to remove the painful lump. He explained, in a manner suitable for my age, how great it would be afterwards for me, how the pain would be less, and I could soon wear my socks and shoes again.

He did not, however, discuss any of the possible complications associated with the surgery. For any other child, this probably would have been a good idea, but for someone who had dealt with so much already, the omission served only to fuel my own fear.

The nurse helped me into a wheelchair, and I was wheeled down the long hallway once more. I felt like the world was spinning. Mom did her best to give me peace of mind and explain to me why the surgery was so important; I knew that the doctors wanted to help me but it didn't make things easier. Dr. Sweetheart, who had seen me before, greeted me in the hallway. He knelt down, held my hand, and listened to my thoughts and fears. Never once did he talk down to me or belittle me. Those few moments where he treated me with the respect I so craved, meant so much to me; the disease had stolen my confidence, and that act of respect helped to restore some of my self-assurance.

In the operating theatre everything was draped in cloths. A tray with various silver surgery instruments sat to my left as I lay on the table. Everyone in the room wore the tell-tale shower caps and masks typical of surgical ward. My ankle was swollen, inflamed, and painful; and at that moment I allowed myself one last glare at the entity that had caused me such grief.

My eyelids grew heavier and rather than fighting to stay awake, I surrendered to the peaceful darkness. When I awoke back in my room, Mom was sitting at the end of the bed reading a book. She looked up, smiled, and came over to the bed to give me hug. I knew everything would be okay after that.

Once the surgery was over, my ankle needed time to heal. Soon the swelling receded, leaving a scar as the only reminder where the lump had been. But being in bed is boring for any kid. I defiantly hung my legs down off the bed but quickly learned that as blood flowed into the foot, it would throb painfully. Each step I took intensified the throbbing sensation, but each day walking brought me one day closer to going back home, so I pushed through the pain.

When I was finally allowed to go home, I tried to keep up with my studies and resume my regular activities, but I became tired easily and required more rest than I had before.

A few days after returning home, my body began to act differently; it shook with chills, and I was sapped of all energy. That night, when Mom changed the bandage on my ankle, my foot was red and hot to the touch. With each step I took, pain shot through my foot that was so severe the painkillers provided no relief – the pain was far worse than anything I'd had before.

We wound up back at the hospital where a nurse, after multiple failed attempts, found a good vein for the intravenous, and eventually an antibiotic surged through my veins.

Every night I was filled with the longing for sleep to blanket my body; but sleep rarely came. I longed for the quiet of my own bedroom and the familiar sounds of the living room and my family. Here the lights from the hallway streamed into my room, and I would be awakened intermittently by the nurses checking on my stubbornly high temperature and my intravenous drip. The medication drained my energy, while the infection raging in my body was reluctant to leave.

A few days later, my vein closed up, and blood flowed back up the intravenous tubing. The nurses, whose faces were usually bright and friendly, were focused and intense. One carried a metal tray draped in a blue cloth which she proceeded to lift off, revealing a needle and some other instruments not familiar to me.

They began to dig away at my veins like riggers drilling for oil. I sat there in a wheelchair with a drainage tube and bandage on one foot and an intravenous tube in the other, before they ultimately had to concede to my inflexible veins, and give me an oral medication instead.

My stay was another blur of constant doctors' visits, assignments, and long, lonely nights. One evening I overheard Dr. Sunshine at the nursing station; I strained to hear the conversation when my name came up.

"Let's keep Alison in a couple of extra days. That'll give her parents a break."

And there it was. With those few words, some of my deepest fears found purchase. My mind scrambled back to the talk of "sending people away." I had heard about it on television.

I have become a burden; I thought. *There might be an ulterior motive to all these hospitalizations after all.*

When my mom came to visit that night, I told her what I had overheard. She reassured me they did not feel that way at all, but to my young mind, what else would she say?

I decided that I needed to keep my behavior in check and make sure to be good, lest the medical team take me away from my family. I began to distrust, rather than simply dislike, my hospitalizations; there could be nothing worse for me than being taken away from my family, the only constant I had in my life.

Chapter Six

The issue of *ulterior motives* took other forms too. A thigh surgery had been scheduled for me that was going to be profiled in a medical journal. Not only was I going to have to endure another painful surgery, but now I was going to be the subject of a whole new set of peering eyes and strangers treating me as an oddity for study.

A *before* photo was to be taken, and I felt extremely self-conscious about it all. As we entered the room a female photographer set up bright lights and a backdrop. Once the lighting had been corrected, I lifted up my skirt to expose the lump in my thigh; to my horror, both my mom and the photographer began to laugh.

"Why are you laughing?" I demanded.

"You have two lovebirds on your socks. It's cute," Mom said.

"I have those at home!" the photographer chimed in. "But don't worry, they won't be in the photograph."

The surgery took place a few days later; and just as with my foot surgery, all that remained of the surgery was a scar and the memories; and of course a journal article complete with photographs. But unlike my foot surgery, the pain during the healing process was far more intrusive; it was impossible for me to sit at all. Lying or standing were the only comfortable positions that provided relief from the pain that throbbed up and down my leg. I felt trapped, a feeling that worsened once the bed's silver metal railings were lifted up on either side, encircling me like a jailer. Due to my lack of muscle strength and joint mobility, even my most persistent efforts to drop one of the railings or climb over the side were wasted. But that didn't stop me from spending some time every day –usually when nightmares woke me – from trying to escape.

At just eight-years-old I had become well-accustomed to the experience of anxiety, even if the word itself was foreign to me. My friends were going to school and taking advantage of extracurricular activities. Their schedules were laid out for them, and other than the odd trip to the dentist, they were not being the victims of a barrage of surprises being hurled at them by their own bodies.

I worried about the strange and weird things this body of mine was doing. I was scared of something I had no control over, scared of the unknown. Each day I awoke feeling almost as tired as when I had gone to bed. My skin burned and ached, and everything moved too quickly. I wanted to yell "stop," to give me time to catch my breath. My body was supposed to work *with* my spirit, instead of battling against it.

When I was discharged following the thigh surgery, we returned home, and I once again became acquainted with a regular schedule. My muscles were more relaxed, and my joints ached less. I completed school work in the mornings while Mom cleaned the house, and in the afternoons we would bake or do crafts together. Some days after school, when Tara didn't have other activities, we would take turns playing at each other's homes.

As the months passed, I had convinced myself my disease had become bored with me and opted for a hibernation period. But no sooner had I lulled myself into a false sense of security, than it awoke and cruelly selected its next target: my left bottom cheek.

This time the red raised lump felt like a rock was embedded underneath my butt cheek; its placement made it impossible for me to avoid. Even with a donut pillow, just sitting built up the pressure and caused such throbbing and unbearable pain that I knew a trip to the clinic was inevitable.

As always, the appointment began with a full examination of my body, and even at that young age I began to feel that their explorations were something of an objectification. The doctors seemed to find my body such a wonder, and I felt as if they thought it was an amusement park through which to go from one spectacle to another. I understood this was all part of keeping my health in check, but the manner, in which these inspections were conducted, particularly with Dr. Pinches, left me feeling violated.

He did not ask my permission before abruptly pulling down both my pants and underwear in one fell swoop, in front of two or three residents. He then proceeded to touch and squeeze the butt cheek, manipulating me to make sure that the interns could all get a good look at my calcification.

I wanted so desperately to pull up my pants, run away, and hide. Of all the examinations I had undergone, all the unwelcome hands touching my body, this one had made me actually feel dirty.

The interns all squatted down and gawked at me as he talked his way through my body as if he was a guide leading an expedition for some great treasure.

And perhaps my medical condition was a source for awe amongst medical students, a *treat* for them to see something that they'd only ever read about in journals. But the fact remained that a young girl stood before them, her underwear around her ankles, her innocence stripped away; my body was not, like the John Mayer song says, "A wonderland." No matter how many baths and showers I took after that day, I couldn't rid myself of the memories of that appointment.

Usually when the calcification lumps popped, they would drain; and life would return to *normal* reasonably soon after – n*ormal* in the sense that I could at least move around in the world with minimal pain and anxiety. But the wait, for this stubborn lump on my bottom to come to a head, seemed endless.

Finally one day, just as I was walking to the front door to bring in the mail, it burst. The sweet-smelling, bloody discharge shot through my clothes and splattered on the floor and walls, running down my leg onto my socks and the floor. I was admittedly embarrassed; but at the same time relief swept through me as I felt an instant relief of the pain. Despite the shock, it was a wonderful relief because the pain lessened. But it also meant that extensive aftercare of the wound would have to be done to prevent another infection. Keeping a bandage dry would undoubtedly be complicated by my upcoming plans.

The summer months were fast approaching. My friends all had plans in the works for how they would be spending the break from school – glorious plans of going on vacations to far away places, or camping out at their lake cabins; but not me.

The sum total of my plans had included studying, in the hopes that I'd be able to earn my passage to the next grade. For me, the school year was no longer ten months; it ran year-round. Even when I could afford to take some time away from the books, my family had learnt early on that making plans was a luxury not afforded us; my disease had a mind of its own.

For the past few years I had been going over to visit our neighbor, Ivy. Her daughter, Grace, was a few years younger than me, but we often enjoyed playing together and going shopping. Grace was just learning to swim; and the more I heard about her adventures in the pool, the more it intrigued me. My therapists were also on board since it would be a great non-weight-bearing exercise for me. There were only two obstacles in my way: my apprehension about my body's own limitations, and convincing Mom and Dad it was a good idea.

In the end, Mom didn't take much convincing at all. She enrolled me in swimming classes at a community pool. Each Saturday I slid my swimsuit on underneath my regular clothes and made the trip to the pool.

The locker room was flanked by tall banks of lockers, and a wooden sauna sat in the far corner. The smell of chlorine, and the dampness of the moisture-filled air hit me, as I walked into the dressing room and removed my outdoor clothes. I walked carefully into the main area and over to the side of the pool. Mom was allowed to sit in the picnic-table area, poolside in case I required assistance.

When the lessons first began, my confidence soared, believing that I would be swimming like a fish by the end of the lessons. After all, all my friends who had taken the same lessons a few years before were now virtual pros.

As the lessons progressed, that excitement morphed into apprehension. Because of my mobility issues, the simple act of moving from a floating position into a standing one proved to be extremely difficult. My balance was even more hindered by the water, and manoeuvring proved impossible, at times. The water was a strong adversary against my legs; I could only float on my back to keep my head above water. My fellow students were quickly surpassing me, floating on both their backs and fronts, and even treading water. Even getting into the pool was a challenge. Before each class, the teacher stepped in ahead of me and supported my back, in case my hands couldn't keep hold of the railing.

By the last class, even though the grading was pass/fail, my overall fearfulness and lack of confidence would not allow me to complete the course successfully.

In a last attempt to push me along, my teacher Buck, a broad and jolly man, wanted me to go under the water and float face down, holding on to his hands. I grabbed hold of his large fingers; as long as I could keep a grip on him, I was more than willing to float upside down.

For the first few seconds, I floated and enjoyed the feeling of weightlessness. I began to feel Buck's hands moving in an attempt to loosen my grip. I hung on with all my might; I wasn't ready to go it on my own. But soon my tiny hands lost their grip; and as Buck pulled his hands up and out of the water, I struggled to reach them.

I tried desperately to right myself in the pool, pulling my legs down and away from the pool surface towards the bottom of the pool. My brain told my legs to get down but the water had other plans. The little bit of air that I had been holding on to was escaping my lungs quickly as I struggled. I fought to get my head out of the water, but my legs continued to float and stubbornly refused to make contact with the bottom. I tried to hold my breath and calm myself down but all the thrashing around left my legs and arms aching.

I heard muffled voices from above the water. I fought the urge to take a breath, but my lungs could not hold on anymore; I gasped. The water rushed up into my nose and burned my lungs.

Someone please help me. I wanted to scream, but couldn't.

Finally, a hand broke through the surface of the water and effortlessly pulled my head up, allowing my feet to find the bottom. For a minute, I was disoriented; coughing and sputtering up the pool water. I pushed frantically against the water, trying to get to the exit. My adrenalin was pumping; and as I reached the edge, I quickly put as much distance between myself and the pool as I could.

I joined Mom at the poolside picnic table where she wrapped me in a large towel and rubbed my back, as I continued coughing up water, trying to catch my breath. My arms, legs, and chest ached. My mom wiped my running nose with a tissue from her purse.

Buck climbed out of the pool, and rushed over to the picnic table. Kneeling down he apologized profusely to me, recognizing his error. But the damage had yet again, already been done. What had once been just a general discomfort with the water had now galvanized into a concrete fear, one that has stayed with me well into adulthood.

As my interest in yet another of the *normal* activities my other friends were engaging in waned, my joy came from the everyday activities I took part in with my family. One day, after getting groceries, I was walking around the mall with my family and stopped to look at the tape recorders. I envied the fact that Cliff was able to use the tape deck in his car to listen to Rock. I loved listening to pop music on my radio, but when my favorite songs were over, they always left me longing for the chance to listen to them again.

To my delight, Mom bought me a black tape deck that not only played cassettes, but also let me record. Until now, my range of music exposure had been limited to Mom, Dad, and Cliff's record collections. Now, with my own player I could finally explore another level of independence. Not only was I able to explore the type of music I wanted, but I could do so in the privacy of my own room, where I was free to belt out the words along with the music.

This simple machine opened up a whole new dimension of expression for me. Music made life more bearable when reality became too much for me. Music and singing allowed me to release all the emotions that burdened me through all my challenges. It gave me freedom.

Chapter Seven

My unstable health, and the increasing challenges of peer interaction, caused my self-confidence to wane – that, along with the intermittent need to use a wheelchair because of joint pain.

The wheelchair was my freedom to be able to go out and explore the world. I had been loaned a wheelchair that was not my size. It was not as comfortable or customizable as a purchased personal wheelchair would be. Although it did restore my freedom, my place within society and the way I was now viewed, was a blow to my self-confidence.

As I searched for my place in a world of people who walked and people who used wheelchairs, Mom looked into the possibility of me attending a class at the local junior high, in an effort to boost my faltering self-esteem. The only classes available to me were electives, but I was grateful for the opportunity. Knowing how much I loved to cook and sew, Home Economics was an easy choice for me. My mother made arrangements for me to begin my very own social experiment.

The hallways were filled with students rushing past, walking and talking as they moved briskly from one class to the next. I forced myself to look up at their faces, wondering what they would see when they looked back. Would they actually see me? Or would they only see a freak, constantly getting in and out of a wheelchair?

But when I met their gazes, they didn't seem to react any differently to me than they did to other students. A tiny spark of hope lit within me as Mom and I ducked into the quiet office to examine the course listing

"The class actually just started. I'll walk you to the room," the receptionist said. She came from behind the counter and escorted us down the hallway and into a classroom with students standing around the scaled-down kitchen areas. The teacher walked over to us, a brightly-colored apron covering her. She was about Mom's age.

"Hello, Alison. We're baking cakes today. How about we put you in a group, and you can join in?"

The teacher walked me over to the middle of the room where a small group of students were gathered around their workspace; with all ovens preheating, the room gave me a legitimate reason for my palms to sweat.

As the students all began to introduce themselves, the lingering lump in my throat began to disappear. There was Frank, tall and athletic, Megan, who was slim and attractive in her flawlessly matching outfit, and Lillian, whose perfectly coiffed do had not one hair out of place. They were focused on the task before them, yet they all seemed to be so carefree and motivated. The students belonged there in that class, in the school – in the world of teenagers. And for those fifty minutes, I would belong there too.

"Warning," Megan said, "we are totally just learning."

"I'm learning – you're making a mess." Frank pointed to the swath of flour covering the counter.

"Alison, have you baked before?" Megan asked.

"Yes!" I replied enthusiastically. One of the benefits of distance education was the fact that I'd had the opportunity to learn other skills, like baking and cooking. And for the first time, those skills were affording me an advantage over all the regular kids, something I would never have dreamt would happen!

"Great. You can help us figure this out," Frank said.

"Students, you have ten minutes to get the cake in the oven," the teacher said.

I was in heaven. Being able to answer their questions, and being looked at as the authority, was something I'd never experienced before. I really did feel like I belonged. Once we'd managed to sort out the recipe, we placed the cake in the oven and cleaned up. As we sat waiting for the buzzer to ring, heralding the completion of our masterpiece, we sat and chatted.

"That assignment is way too long. Mr. Smith is impossible," Megan said.

"Oh please. You should try Mrs. Johnson! You should see the ridiculously long and boring book he's making us read and write a report on," Frank said.

"What do you think?" Megan looked at me; I realized that she had no idea that I wasn't one of the regular students.

"Oh, those assignments are really something!" I said, wishing I had some remote idea about the curriculum they were dealing with. This was my way of searching for a way to contribute to the discussion, and keep up the illusion that I was just a regular everyday junior high student.

The room began to fill with the aroma of vanilla and chocolate as each group began to pull their culinary creations out of the oven. The teacher soon came by, cut a slice of our chocolate cake, inspected it and took a bite, "Light, fluffy. An A+."

"Yes!" we all exclaimed, giving each other a celebratory high five.

I was laughing. I was learning. I was fitting in with a group of people whom just a few minutes ago had been perfect strangers.

For that hour and a half of my life I was more than a disease, more than a wheelchair. I was Alison, a thirteen-year-old girl who was learning how to bake. But no sooner had we completed our self-congratulations, than the bell rang. Class was over; and it was time for the other students to move on to the next section of their schedules, and for me to return to my solitary existence.

"Did you enjoy yourself?" Mom asked me, on the way home.

"I did; I was treated like a normal student!"

"Of course, honey. You are normal. You just get around differently."

It's always one thing for your mother to assuage your fears; that's their job. But having been a party to the day's events finally allowed me to see that beyond the safe confines of my home and the loving arms of my family, others saw me as *normal* too. As the months went by, my participation in the class afforded me all the opportunities I could have wanted, not only to grow my cooking and baking skills, but also to engage in the kind of social interactions I had so craved.

The family enjoyed all the recipes and baking homework the classes presented me, and the sewing instruction allowed me to bond with Mom in yet another way. She'd always been an avid sewer. She would take just a few scraps of fabric and transform them into beautiful dresses for me in just a few hours. And while the sewing remained a challenge for me – my arthritic fingers making it hard for me to hold the needle and cut fabric – I was able to share my growing love for the medium.

One evening Mom and I were in the kitchen making apple turnovers, when all of a sudden sharp pains shot through my chest and stomach. Thinking it was my stomach revolting on me, I tried to ease the pain with a glass of milk.

"Are you okay? The color's just run out of your face," Mom asked.

She knew me too well. I could try and manage my reaction to discomfort, to mask it. But there was nothing I could do to prevent my face from growing pale.

"My chest hurt, but the milk made it feel better. I'm fine." I tried to brush it off as no big deal.

"That's good honey, but if it's not better by morning, we should contact the doctor."

"Mom, it's probably nothing. Please don't mention it."

But as I climbed into bed, the chest pain jabbed into my chest like an electric shock, each time growing stronger than before. Another glass of milk provided me with temporary comfort, but it was short-lived. I couldn't hide my concern from Mom any longer, and she scheduled a trip to see Dr. Sunshine the next morning.

The usual examination revealed that the doctors suspected both pneumonia and an ulcer. And while I should have been devastated or at least shocked, the sad fact is that I wasn't. I'd almost become resigned to yet another hospitalization.

I'd almost become blasé; I felt relatively confident since Dr. Sunshine would be treating me, and he had always included me in all discussions, and always made me feel like I was an active part of my treatment.

But that night my chest began to tighten and my heart was being kneaded like bread dough; for the first time in a while I began to feel truly frightened. Mom was just about to leave for the night when a sensation like nothing I had ever experienced before thundered deep in my chest.

Mom quickly went in search of a doctor.

"Mom, it's late. You can go home."

"Are you sure? I feel bad leaving you before the doctor comes."

"I'm all right, and besides I'm in a hospital. There's lots of help if I need it." I did all I could to keep my feelings of fear from being reflected in my eyes.

It took some convincing, but she eventually put on her coat and gave me a hug.

"If you need me, feel free to call," she whispered.

She walked out of the room, then returned just a minute later.

"The nurse says it shouldn't be long before the doctor comes. Try to have a good night's sleep."

I nodded.

Mom gave me another hug then disappeared down the hallway.

I lay in silence, trying desperately to get comfortable, despite the pain in my chest. Just as I had succumbed to the quiet, my rest was disturbed in the early morning hours by a hoard of voices in my room.

I peeled open my eyes, with some difficulty, when a doctor turned on my bedside light and began flipping through pages in my file. I fought to keep my eyes open and stay present.

He examined me, turned the light off, pulled the curtain back, and exited the room as quickly as he had entered.

The next morning, a nurse wheeled me downstairs past the nursery packed full of babies in cribs. On one side the room I saw all the premature babies. Their tiny size made them look almost inhuman – like Barbie dolls. But some were even smaller, no bigger than my hand. The nurse parked me in the waiting room, where I sat alone. The rising sun had lent an orange and pink hue to the clouds, bringing me a small degree of hope that today might be better than yesterday had been.

A woman in a long lab coat checked my identification bracelet before wheeling me into a semi-dark room. After she helped me onto the bed, a cool gel was squeezed onto my chest. The ultrasound machine was brought over, and its little balled wand was rolled along my chest, rendering images of my heart to the monitor. The technician allowed me to see the images as they were produced and I found it entertaining to watch for a while. But I found myself wanting to know exactly what it was they were looking for; I wanted to give the predator that was stalking me a shape or a name – something tangible I could focus my energies on fighting.

When I returned to my room, Mom was there to help me get the sticky gel washed off and change me back into my own clothes. Before long, the doctor came to see us.

"Alison has fluid around the heart. Sometimes we need to insert a needle into the fluid sack in order to drain it…"

As my mind visualized a massive needle poking into the image I had seen in the monitor just a few minutes earlier, I was sure that my heart had actually stopped.

"…but we think the steroids will clear it up."

Relief washed over me. There are few things more terrifying than the idea of a large pointy object being stabbed into your chest. And as the doctor left, Mom and I both heaved a huge sigh of relief. The steroid treatment proved effective, and while my hospital stay meant I would miss out on that week's Home Ec. class, my absence was brief, and I was able to resume attending classes well before the end of term.

I was released – with a new special diet designed to allow my stomach time to heal – and returned home just in time for my 14th birthday. This year in particular, we all marvelled at the fact that no-one on my medical team had thought I would even live this long.

In celebration, I had asked my parents to allow me to have a few friends sleep over. Mom set up the air mattress beside the twin beds in my room, and Tara and Grace came over for an evening of typical teenage girl fun. We sat in my bedroom, listened to music, and painted our nails.

"Dave is so hot. We're all going out to a movie next week." Tara smiled. "You should come, too."

"Maybe." I said.

"Mr. K's essays are brutal," Grace looked at Tara.

"He always asks too much of us," Tara said.

Searching for Normal
Alison Neuman

"Ooh, I finally got a raise!" Tara exclaimed, "Now I'm going to buy that amazing jacket I was talking about."

"Having more spending cash is essential if you want to go out," Grace added.

Even on topics as basic as these, I found myself increasingly unable to participate. Grace and Tara shared a common bond based simply on the fact that they were attending regular schools and socializing with students our age on a daily basis. I was experiencing a reality that was completely different than theirs. True, we all had to deal with curricula and schoolwork. But their lives involved the social activities that a stable life afforded. My life felt like it revolved around my health, and my medications.

I was stuck somewhere between being a child and being a teenager. When I had my disease-trapped-me at the hospital or the house, I would play with my dolls and toys, write stories in my head, and try to adapt to the situations my disease created. This coping measure made me seem immature, and made it seem like I was existing in a world completely different from my friends. But the reality is – I was.

In many ways, I had been forced to grow up so much more quickly than my friends could imagine. What some might have considered *childish* elements of my personality had, in fact, allowed me to cope with the very adult experiences of isolation and upheaval I'd been faced with.

In the wee hours of the morning, everyone else in the bedroom had drifted off to a peaceful sleep. Sleep rarely brought me any joy or comfort, and as my friends drifted off, my happiness faded. Nightmares often roused me abruptly and once awake, getting back

63

to sleep was always impossible. This night was no different. I lay quietly in my bed, trying to fall back to sleep; a feeling of hopelessness tested my patience. I looked at my friends and wondered for a moment if their dreams ever resembled mine? Was I even *normal* in that respect? Did terrifying dreams haunt them at night; waking them, and leaving their hearts racing? If they did, they certainty didn't show it.

When my friends went home the next day, silence filled my room; and I felt more alone than I had before. Time by myself gave me time to think – way too much time to think. I tried not to think about the *what-ifs*, knowing that I could never see the future or change the past. When things were going well, I always waited for something bad to crop up, because something always did.

Several important milestones accompanied the advent of my 14th birthday – the first being Mom and Dad's decision to finally allow me to have a pet of my very own. We'd had budgies, but in my eyes, they hardly counted as pets. No, this time it would be a rabbit. Something I could actually hold, and interact with – a creature whose care was going to be my responsibility. And that creature took the form of a brown dwarf rabbit, ringed with a strip of white around his neck and a matching patch on its foot.

"Would you like to hold him?" the pet store employee asked.

"Yes," I said as a smile spread across my face.

She walked into the back room and picked up the tiny bunny. She came back and gently placed it in my arms; it snuggled into the crook of my lap, and looked up with sparkly brown eyes.

"He's the one."

"I definitely think he's the one," Mom said, petting his soft fur.

On the ride home, I held him close and dubbed him "Sparky."

That evening we sat in the living room, and I brought Sparky over to introduce him to Cliff, who was dressed for work in a white sweater and fancy dress pants. He lay down on the orange-shag living room carpet and cuddled the tiny bunny on his chest. And then...

"Sparky!! You didn't just?" Cliff exclaimed. "Ew!"

Cliff looked up at me and scowled.

"Alison, come get Sparky. He just peed all over my new sweater."

As Cliff gently handed me Sparky, I couldn't help but laugh hysterically at him and the bright yellow patch that now adorned his shirt – and neither could he.

Sparky's arrival seemed to signal a new phase in my life. Once my stomach had healed, my heart had straightened out, and my life became more or less regular again, I was enjoying the security of regular schedules and being at home – even though it still meant not attending school with my peers. I was almost relaxed, and had even embraced the idea that my disease might be going into remission. The calcifications no longer seemed interested in choosing new locations from which to erupt; my body seemed to have more energy; my hips seemed to have greater mobility; and even math seemed to be a little bit less of a struggle than before.

And then along came the rite of passage that every teen dreams of. All of my friends couldn't wait to get their learners' permits and be able to drive a car. Of all my friends, I had been the first to turn fourteen, and be eligible to write the permit test. Even though I wasn't sure whether my hips or legs would allow me to really drive a car, I figured that since it was only a written test, I wasn't going to let my body get in the way of this landmark event in every teenager's life.

Every day, I spent time memorizing the study guide from front to back. When the day came to write it, I sat myself down at the computer in the licensing office. One by one, I read each question and pondered the answers. At first, it seemed far too simple – this couldn't possibly be all there was to it, could it? With each answer entered, the computer announced my success and failures on the screen. My palms suddenly began to sweat when a red X appeared on the screen – only so many incorrect answers were allowed. But before another 'X' was able to appear, the words "Pass" appeared on the screen.

In that moment my disease, my arthritis hadn't been able to conquer me, and as I walked over to the counter to fill in the paperwork and have my photograph taken, Mom watched me, beaming.

Minutes later, permit in my hand, I was licensed to drive a car with a licensed driver present. Not that I really had any intention to do so, but that wasn't the point – it never had been.

Chapter Eight

Thinking about the idea of driving had served to highlight how much my hips had now become a growing concern for me at this point. I realized that something needed to be done, that I needed to get help, because increasingly, my body was building up a resistance to the pain medication. I was needed higher and higher doses of the meds, and I was getting less and less relief each time. My life was back on hold; those few normal activities that I had fought so hard to retain in my life were now slipping from my grasp.

So there we found ourselves once again – sitting in the emergency room, waiting hour after hour in a single-bed examining room. The emergency nurses were growing increasingly frustrated with Dr. Cowboy as he had not returned their calls asking for permission to administer medication. After four or five hours, Dr. Cowboy abruptly opened the door and stomped into the room. His shoulders were pulled back, and he wasn't in one of his usual fancy suits; his face was stiff and long.

"What do you expect me to do?" Dr. Cowboy yelled at Mom.

No adult was ever allowed to raise their voice to another adult, let alone a child, in my home. My hips were throbbing, my stomach was churning, and tears filled my eyes. I wondered if everyone in the emergency heard him. I wondered why Mom was just sitting there, letting him talk to her in such a matter. Then he turned around in front of me.

"If we do surgery on her," he said, "she will bleed to death."

And with that he stormed out of the room.

I blinked and tried to process what had just happened, to absorb what he had just said. Mom sat in stunned silence for several minutes. We both looked at each other, and back at the door trying to wrap our heads around what we'd just seen. I couldn't understand why we were being punished like this. Yes, I'm sure it was frustrating for the doctor, not having a way to *fix* my problems, but it wasn't my fault. Nor was it my mom, Dad, or Cliff's fault.

My heart pounded – not only at the fact that he had been so heartless, but at the thought that seemed to be no end in sight to my pain, that no one was going to help us.

"Mom, I'm sorry. If my hip wasn't so bad, you wouldn't have to put up with this." Teardrops ran down my face.

She looked at me, stood up, and gave me a hug.

"Honey, it's not your fault."

Soon a nurse came in with some medication.

"Alison," she said, "we finally got the orders to give you something for pain."

She turned to my mom.

"Are you okay? We could hear him in the hallway. His behavior and his attitude was completely uncalled for."

"I'm okay," Mom said, but I could see the tears in her eyes.

"Alison, this'll make you feel better. An orderly is going to take you for X-rays soon to ensure your joints are okay."

The results of the X-rays indicated that my hip joints were completely engulfed with arthritis; and I was hospitalized in the hopes they could find a treatment protocol that would work for me. The weeks passed though, and nothing changed. Not a single new treatment was embarked upon, and repeated attempts by the staff to contact Dr. Cowboy failed; no one knew where he was.

The hospital schedule and routines were becoming far too familiar and my sense of isolation grew rapidly. The pain meds never provided me with complete relief; they just dropped the pain down to a seven from a ten. At times I shook violently and shivered from the severity of the pain. It was the worse stint in hospital I could remember. And it took an even worse turn with the introduction of *Nurse Dictator*.

Nurse Dictator's first appearance saw her striding in my room, hands on her hips.

"Alison," she declared, "on doctor's orders, we're limiting your family visits to evenings only."

Before I could even absorb that phrase, she began rummaging through my clean clothes and started picking out an outfit and socks. I wanted to question why on earth they'd be eliminating the time I spent with the only people who made me feel safe and secure.

"Shower time," she declared.

"Thanks, but tonight Mom's giving me a shower."

"You're having one now."

She walked over to the door, put her hands on her hips again, and stood there waiting until I followed her to the shower room down the hallway.

Who did this woman think she was? She was treating me like I was some puppet she could pull and move around in whatever direction she chose.

In the shower room, she set my clothes on the table and spun around to face me.

"Do you need help in the shower?"

"No thanks, I'm good." *You'd be the last person I'd want touching me.*

She walked out of the room, and I locked the door behind her. I knew that the shower room could be opened in an emergency, so really I wasn't totally safe; but just for the moment I was at least invisible to her prying eyes.

With the door locked, I wet my hair, changed my clothes and waited until I thought enough time had passed. This time in hospital had left me feeling like a bug in a jar, and for those few moments I was locked in the bathroom, there was no one there poking me, prodding me – no one tapping on the glass to see how I'd react.

As Nurse Dictator had predicted, my family visits were now limited to just evenings. The days were long and stretched out between intern visits, rest periods, the playroom, and schoolroom. My hips began to improve as a new anti-inflammatory treatment resulted in fewer episodes and less pain. Soon, my favorite words rolled off a nurse's lips: discharge. And after five long weeks, we were packing up my stuff to leave for good.

We left the ward and traveled down the elevator to the main entrance where our ride was waiting; the tension that had been stored up in my body was released, and I felt as though an incredible weight had been lifted off me. Tears of joy welled up in my eyes.

"Honey, are you okay?" Mom looked at the tears in my eyes.

"I thought I'd never get out of there."

"It's all over now. Soon you will be home," she assured me, wrapping me in her arms.

But despite the new medications, my hips and knees were still painful; and just walking aggravated them. With no promise of the arthritis going into remission, I was now going to have to use a wheelchair.

The wheelchair gave me mobility and freedom; but relying on it, and being dependent on it to get around, took getting used to. Even more than that, finding the right wheelchair was, in itself, something that took a lot of work.

Buying a wheelchair is very much like shopping for new a car and in essence, these would be my new wheels! Just like getting a car, there are dozens of options available and a myriad of variables at play – manual or electric – lightweight or sturdy – fold-up or standard – blue or silver?

Finally, we made the decision to get me a fold-up manual chair that would fit easily into our car – and most importantly, in blue.

A few weeks later we went to the hospital to pick it up. The door opened before me, and there sat a shiny blue wheelchair.

"Take her for a test drive," my physiotherapist said.

Mom helped me transfer into the new chair. It fit better than anything I'd tried before. It allowed me space between my thighs and the sides of the chair; and my legs extended to allow my feet to comfortably fit in the footrests. I could push it far more easily than those I'd used at the hospital, and it made for a much more comfortable ride.

"What do you think?" the physiotherapist asked me.

"It's perfect. Thank you."

But while the physical issues associated with using a wheelchair were proving minimal, the psychological ones were more difficult to overcome. The day the wheelchair became my legs, my identity changed from being a *walker* to being a *sitter*. I was the same person I'd been before, but now the outside world saw and treated me differently. Not only was it an adjustment for me, but for everyone in the family, and all my friends.

On one warm summer evening, Mom and I decided to go over to our local Dairy Queen to get an ice cream. Dad was mowing the lawn. He turned the mower off, when we started heading down the sidewalk.

"Bill, we're going to walk to get an ice cream. Would you like one?"

He looked at Mom and me for a moment, silent.

"Does she really need to take the wheelchair?" he asked.

"Alison needs the wheelchair to get around, Bill," Mom said.

"But someone might see her in the wheelchair," Dad said.

72

And at that moment, my heart sunk deep into my chest. How could he not understand how important it was for me to be able to get out, to experience life instead of living in some tiny corner of the house watching the world pass by? *Ability was all that mattered.*

But I realized that I was still adjusting to having the wheelchair as a permanent attachment as well. His little girl's whole world had changed, and he had to adapt to her new identity. And in time, he did. In fact, he ended up being the one who helped open up the world to me even more.

While I didn't have an overwhelming number of activities requiring travel, accessibility was an issue; and many places – including our own home – became a challenge to navigate. The simple act of Dad building and installing ramps allowed me to start exploring the world and venturing out on my own again.

But there are some things that we can't build our way out of; and winter was one of them. As the snow pilled up, collecting on sidewalks and ramp, I began to experience a growing feeling of confinement. Just for me to leave the house, someone would have to go outside and shovel. And if any melting and freezing had occurred on the ramp, then we had to wait until the afternoon, when the ice had melted a bit to make our passage safer. For much of the winter, the streets in front of our house were so thick with snow that cars generally found themselves either stuck or careening sideways. And while the city was good about removing snow from the main drags, only when it got *really* bad, did they plow the residential streets where we lived.

Eventually, cabin fever set in.

"Mom, I need to go outside. I feel trapped. Even if we just sit on the front step, I need to be outside."

"I understand. Let's get dressed up, and give it a try."

We put on our warmest clothes, and she pushed me out the front door. The snow on the front stoop crunched under the pressure of my wheels. The cool air brushed against my face.

Ah, freedom.

Snow banks several feet high lined the edges of streets and sidewalks all around us. Having made it down our ramp, we ventured down the main sidewalk. But soon my wheelchair began to struggle as it advanced on the newly fallen wet snow. Then my front tire stuck and became jammed – I might as well have had the brakes on. My wheelchair began to tip forward, and the jolt caused an ache to thump through my body.

"I don't think we can go anywhere," Mom said.

Agreeing with her, we turned to go home but instead, the tire jammed once again stubbornly. We couldn't move forward, we couldn't go back. We were stuck.

Realizing we were stranded just ten feet from home I began to giggle.

"I wonder if we could call a tow truck," I said, and mom began to laugh hysterically.

"Alison, stop laughing. I can't push when I'm laughing."

"Sorry."

I continued laughing as we contemplated the need for *AMA wheelchair-towing* services.

Chapter Nine

Throughout the course of my education, the need for distance learning had meant that the school experience had generally been an exercise in solitude. It isolated me in more ways than just physically; I was studying a different curriculum than my friends, making the opportunities that came from sharing the frustrations and joys of completing each assignment with classmates, unavailable to me.

Beyond academics, the social aspects encompassed in going to school as a fourteen-year-old, were foreign to me. I still found my daily schedule so dramatically difficult from my friends' that when we did manage to visit, the number of common experiences we could share grew to be fewer and fewer.

By Grade Seven this isolation, coupled by my need to take additional medications for pain management, as well as the growing intensity of course requirements, found me intensely frustrated. Nowhere did this frustration become more severe than when dealing with math.

After my Grade Two experience, my confidence had taken a blow from which I'd never fully recovered. My resentment only grew when I recognized that one of the only ways to ensure my success going forward was to get off the pain meds that kept my brain in a fog – and this wasn't an option at all.

75

An in-house tutor came twice a week to provide one-on-one support, but still I struggled.

The exams for distance education classes were always scheduled for mornings in order to accommodate the need for extended time allotments. Despite the anxiety that accompanies anyone when approaching writing an exam, I actually looked forward to test days. Because, for me, exam day meant a *girls day out* for Mom and me. After the exams, we would explore the shopping centers and movie theatres that sat just a few blocks from the correspondence office.

We set off to the test site early on a late spring morning, me with my pens, pencils, and good luck charms in tow. Mom wheeled me into the testing room, and I opened up the test booklet.

Staring at it blankly for a moment, I tried to recall the course information. Outside the window, traffic rushed along the street, and off in the distance, it echoed its way through the many tall buildings. Daydreaming, I found myself crossing the stage to accept my high school diploma, going on a date, working – just participating in an average, everyday life activity. My daydreams were interrupted when an employee poked her head in the door.

"Is everything going alright?"

"Yes, thanks," I answered, grateful for the reminder that if I did not complete these exams, there would be zero possibility of any of my daydreams coming true.

With the door closed, the quiet surrounded me and encouraged me to focus on the task at hand. I worked steadily for the next several hours until finally, after a quick check over all the questions I left the room, booklet in hand. I wheeled over to the noisy main counter where the employee met me and asked the same question they always did.

"How did it go?"

"Either great or poorly," was my scripted response.

"It was one of those exams."

After signing the exam booklet, Mom and I were free for our day out. After every exam, I found myself in conflict; I felt relief that the course was over, but I always worried whether my efforts would be reflected in my grades.

A warm, gentle breeze circulated between buildings on our eight block walk to the shopping centre. The city was vacant of the large snowdrifts and wind chills that had trapped my wheelchair a few months prior, and I traced our progress down the sidewalk, noting the landmarks as we passed.

Pedestrians passed us on either side. Professionals, dressed in suits and dresses, carried their briefcases along the sidewalks as they made their way towards their destinations. A hint of exhaust from the cars lingered in the air, broken by the intermittently planted trees and flowers that kept the urban center feeling less like a concrete jungle. The sound of engines, and the click of Mom's shoes as they met the sidewalk, echoed between the tall buildings.

Finally we ended up at the entrance to the shopping area and left the urban rush behind. Inside, the fluorescent lighting of shop signs highlighted the countless products all vying for our attention. Inside the department store restaurant, one of our traditional stops, an elderly hostess led us over to a table with four chairs. She removed one of the comfy high-backed burgundy chairs, and Mom parked my wheelchair in its space. In the middle of the table was a candle in a small red glass holder that shone the flame's dancing lights onto the table. For Mom and me, this was a lunch worthy of candle-lighting; it was a celebration of completing Grade Seven.

Once settled, the waitress snapped her gum while she filled Mom's coffee. Her nails were painted with a fire engine red nail polish.

"Red is your Dad's color," Mom remarked, smiling after the waitress left.

"Dad doesn't wear nail polish." I grinned at her.

"One evening Auntie Helen came over when your Dad was sleeping on the couch. Helen was painting her nails red, and I said, 'Oh, we should paint one of Bill's nails.'"

"You didn't?" I said incredulously.

"It was just the thumb. But he went to work and didn't even notice."

Tears collected in Mom's eyes as her laughter flowed out. Just picturing my serious-looking father walking down the street in bright red nail gloss made me burst out laughing, until I too, could no longer contain the tears.

"Mom, what happened when he got to work?"

"Aww, he saw it on the walk to work and scraped it off before he got there. So not quite as funny as it could have been!"

It was one of those stories that remind you that your parents are actually *people* – that they had an entire existence before we came along. They had regular lives of growing up, working, dating, and getting married. I'm always grateful for those little snapshots of their lives that remind me of how goofy and loving my parents are, beyond their relationship with us. And they always serve as a reminder that if I can be even a quarter of the Mom, the friend, the woman she is, then maybe I might grow up okay.

The addition of basic cable to our household provided me with an interesting catalyst. Cliff decided to get the add-on of Much Music – the twenty-four hour video channel that defined a generation of 80s kids. Music had always been a constant in my life, but the addition of Much Music sparked something me – it became something of a soundtrack to my life in the house.

During one of our weekly supper and game evenings, Mom, Dad, my uncle Ingmar and I were at the dining room table in the middle of a game. With Dad's permission, we were listening to Much Music instead of the usual Emeralds and Statler Brother's records that were part of the regular rotation in our home. I turned to my family and referred to the singer on television.

"I'm going to do that one day. Be a singer … make music … perform on stage."

Mom, Dad and Uncle Ingmar glanced at each other and smiled.

Dad began laughing.

My heart sank.

"No, I am! Just watch me."

Mom stopped smiling, and rubbed her hand on mine. They all softened when they realized my comment was not meant as a joke, but as a declaration of intent. I realized that it had come as a bit of a shock to them all – I think I had even shocked myself a bit, saying it out loud. It's one thing to sing in the shower, but being competent enough to sing and perform onstage is a whole other level. I couldn't read music, and playing an instrument had never been possible with the limitations my arthritis presented. But I found solace in the fact that every singer, musician, or songwriter had to start from somewhere. Many of them faced challenges, but they all had a moment from which they began to surmount those obstacles. This would be my beginning.

In the days that followed my sudden proclamation, I searched for a formula to help achieve my dream of being a singer. Realizing how profound my new-found passion had grown, Mom shared her own teenage dream with me during afternoon tea.

She told me a story of how she and two other students had formed a trio. Mom sang alto, another girl soprano, and the third girl played piano. One of their teachers had heard them play during recess and invited them to sing at the Christmas program. They performed one song to thunderous applause, necessitating several encores and invitations from the community for additional performances.

My heart filled with joy to know that my mother and I shared this passion for music; she understood my dream at a level no one else did.

"Why didn't you pursue it professionally?" I set my cup down in anticipation of the answer.

"Our piano player moved out of town with her folks. My friend and I still sang once in awhile, but we never bothered with anything serious. That's the way life goes sometimes."

Mom took an encouraging sip of her tea, and we sat quietly together. I contemplated how appropriate that story was, and how it just might be the sign I had been looking for.

Soon it was fall, and my friends were buying school supplies and preparing for the upcoming school year, some with absolute dread and others with excitement. I wanted desperately to attend junior high full-time, to experience having real teachers and, more importantly, to be with other students. My hopes were cautiously high. A wheelchair had now replaced my legs as my means of mobility, and I wondered if the public school system had room for me this time.

Mom took on the challenge of finding a wheelchair accessible school – we needed a school that was open both to my difference and to my potential. My dream school –one that included a focus on writing and music – existed, but was shot down immediately due to inaccessibility. Mom was positive there was a school that would accommodate me, but my heart broke to think that my mobility, or its limitations, would be the deciding factor in our choice.

Every afternoon Mom picked up the phone book and began to call the junior high schools across the city. And every afternoon she was told there was no room for her daughter. Each day brought more negative replies. No one had the facilities to accommodate my wheelchair. No one wanted *special*. No one wanted *different*. Schools all wanted *normal*.

Finally, one junior high school welcomed me and was eager to have us come in to register the following day. They not only had the facilities to meet my needs, but also had other students with different mobility requirements, and an aide that could help with personal care. So one week into regular classes, we made the trip to the school; the orange and red leaves were falling off the trees and floating in the breeze. I treated every new landmark on the drive to school as a monument to our victory.

When we arrived at the school and its carefully manicured lawns, Mom loaded me into my wheelchair and we made our way up the concrete pad and through the brown wooden doors that squeaked an announcement of our arrival. We had gotten there just at a break between classes, and students crowded through the hallways; new noises and new faces surrounded me on every side. We caught our breath in the safety and silence of the office.

"This is Alison, and we are here to register," Mom said as I absorbed the words and smiled to myself.

"I'll call the aide to come meet you," the secretary replied.

Mom and I sat, filling in the paperwork, and then we waited. My mind was flooded with questions. Will I get along with the aide? Will my wheelchair be an issue with students? Will I be able to break through the medication haze and get the grades I craved? And ultimately, the most important question – would my disease allow me to do any of this?

Before letting self-doubt creep in, I pushed all these questions out of my mind with a resounding *yes*.

Please let me like her. A short, muscular woman entered the office, and smiled in our direction. She took us on a tour of the school and explained what her other student required, and how the first day would go. Almost immediately, we clicked; and my confidence grew knowing that with her help, many of the seemingly *simple* activities other students didn't think twice about – things like brushing my hair, going to the washroom, writing –wouldn't limit my success. We left the school, and as we headed out to purchase school supplies, just like all my other friends, I became increasingly excited for the next day.

We started out early the next morning, the painkillers and breakfast already in my system, and I tuned the radio of our old brown Dodge to a station that would appropriately serve as the soundtrack to my new adventure. The ride there flew by, and as Mom unloaded me and my wheelchair, my aide stood waiting for me by the door.

"Good luck. Have a good day," Mom said, giving me a hug.

"Thanks. I will," I said confidently. But I was surprised to find that when the knowledge of her absence really hit me, I felt a stab of pain in my heart. Barring my very intermittent elementary school experiences, we had shared nearly every little moment together. But if something exciting happened here, I would have no one to share it with until she picked me up after school.

The aide pushed me to my locker and helped me slide off my coat. Then she wheeled me to my homeroom where I sat beside a desk in the front row and waited for class to begin. It was clear almost immediately that my homeroom teacher, Mr. T – a tall, cool man who also served as my social studies teacher – was one who strove to make learning fun. On the first day a pretty girl named Lucy sat beside me in homeroom, and we hit it off almost instantly. And by the end of the first week, I had met another fascinating girl, Zinnia, who I became fast friends with. She was an amazing person, so petite and with such a sweet spirit; and she sat next to me.

"There's something all my friends need to know," she said.

"I'm perfect."

It was the best ice-breaker I'd heard, and it sealed the deal between us.

During that first week, the school held its student government elections. The Grade Eight class needed a representative, and I thought it would be a great experience to try and run. The application process required that we collect five student, and three teacher signatures to nominate the applicant. After a few classes, I proudly handed in my form with all the required signatures.

Lucy offered to be my campaign manager, and she worked with me creating and sticking up posters. And just a few short days later, before I knew it, the announcement came over the intercom:

"Congratulations to Alison Neuman, our new Grade Eight representative."

Just a couple of weeks into the school year, and already I had carved myself a path into junior high *normalcy*.

I looked forward to every lunch hour council meeting – and like most students, even more so to the lucky occasions where we were allowed to miss class. The council voted on matters regarding dances and social events for the student body – many of which we were expected to attend. Attending school was finally becoming the social activity I had always hoped it would be.

Of course, there were still doctors' appointments to attend. But unlike other students who hoped to skip a full day for a trip to the dentist, I would schedule them for as late in the school day as possible. At one of the appointments, they suggested that I get an electric wheelchair to provide me with greater independence. And fortunately, since the cost of a motorized chair was beyond my family's budget, they would provide us with the necessary funding.

But before I would be allowed to have an electric wheelchair full-time, I had to log *road time*. So during my class's gym time, while fellow students were playing basketball, I worked behind the yellow curtain on the stage in an effort to make myself road-worthy.

Rule number one was to NEVER use high speed when people were around, as tempting as it might be. Using the joystick-like button to control the chair took some practice; I was jerking and swaying as I tried to navigate the wheelchair smoothly around objects without getting whiplash. A slight push on the joystick, and the wheelchair jerked forward just like flooring the gas pedal in a car.

But my days playing Burgertime on my old Intellivision were coming in handy, and all the practice started to pay off. Negotiating sharp turns was exhilarating when the tires squealed on the newly waxed floor. Moving around this freely, without having to depend on someone else was liberating – as liberating as learning to walk.

My friends had all begun dating, most often at social events like the school dances. It was all foreign territory to me, though, and I still didn't feel entirely comfortable with the prospect. But as it happened, I had encountered a boy in my homeroom who seemed to live a life that, like me, was different from the rest of our fellow students. Now while our circumstances weren't the same, we did share a couple of commonalities that set us apart from other students. He and I were always in our homeroom a good forty minutes before classes started – me so I could meet with my aide and she would have time to help the other student, and him so that he could be somewhere he felt safe. His home was not that place; he just wanted a place where he could feel secure to sleep, study, or just be a kid. He was pretty quiet but he and I would often chat. We got around to talking about an upcoming school dance one day, and we'd decided that we were going to get together to dance at the event.

When the day of the dance finally arrived I found myself once again far apart from the crowd. Instead of being down on the gym dance floor, I was up on the stage, alone, watching. I was only half present; at the dance, but not really participating. I waited for the boy to come find me and get that promised dance, but he never appeared.

I spoke to him a few days later we spoke and he told me he had looked, but hadn't been able to find me, but I knew he couldn't have been telling me the truth. I was on the stage, after all – pretty darn easy to spot. I was devastated. It didn't have anything to do with me needing to be dating a boy in order to validate my existence, but it signified just another aspect of *normal* everyday life that was being closed off to me. My aide could see I was upset and told me not to take it personally, that while he probably didn't have an issue with my wheelchair that his friends might. That he might have feared being teased by his friends. But that hardly made me feel any better about things. I was being judged by something I had no control over – a difference I could do nothing to change. How was anyone going to get to know the real me if they couldn't even get past my wheelchair?

Junior High was becoming a successful venture, by my standards. My academic efforts finally began to be rewarded, when after science class the teacher approached me.

"Alison," he said, "you are doing great. You have a mark of 99%. Congratulations."

I was greeted with high fives from my friends in the hallway who had overheard the remark; pride filled my body, and my heart skipped a beat. At lunch I even had students who were complete strangers approach my table.

"Are you the student who has 99% in science?" they asked, enviously.

"Yes, I am," I responded proudly.

As things in my academic and social life began to fall into place, I was still faced with the reality of regular appointments with my specialist. On one occasion, we were called into the examining room where Dr. Pinches promptly proceeded to traumatise me once again by parading my body in front of residents – pinching every new and old calcification across my body, in both public and private areas. He left the room, and Mom helped me get dressed and collect some of my dignity. Then Dr. Pinches stampeded back into the room and abruptly announced.

"Violet, come with me. Alison, once we are done talking, you can leave."

We gave each other a look, and Mom left the room.

Mom returned silently into the room a few minutes later, and silently helped me on with my coat. She was vacant of any particular expression or body language indicating what they might have discussed. My heart raced and my mind swirled wondering what painful procedure he might have in store.

At the hospital front entrance we waited for our cab and discussed anything but what was said in their private discussion. While the suspense was killing me, I wanted to hold off on asking her until we were in the comfort of familiar, safe surroundings.

"What did the doctor tell you? I finally blurted out, unable to wait. "It's bad news, isn't it?"

Mom met my gaze.

"Maybe we should discuss this at home."

I knew she was probably right, but we were the only two people around.

"Mom, it's my body. Can you please tell me now?"

She grabbed my hand and squeezed it,

"Honey, the doctors want to put you in the hospital to wean you off the steroids."

"For how long?"

"Two to three months. But you'll have your entire life ahead of you when you are discharged."

"My entire life? But all my plans ..." I struggled to absorb what she'd said.

Mom gazed outside the window as if searching for our cab or perhaps a distraction, something that would make the news more palatable.

She looked back at me.

"If something isn't done now," she said plainly, "they think you won't live to be twenty."

She gathered me in a hug as the words filtered through the sanitized air, and sunk into my brain.

Sure, the doctors had used the word 'terminal' before – but not recently. I still had so many things left to accomplish. I wanted to sing, graduate, learn to drive, go to Disneyland, fall in love, and deepen my relationships with friends and family.

Time – I needed more time.

I knew this hospital admission would give me the time I needed, but still my spirit was wounded at the thought of leaving everything I had worked so hard to build.

Ultimately, I realized that after months of cramps, pain, bloating, and losing pieces of myself to the disease that continued to stalk me, that it was the only option. So as the inevitable preparations for hospitalization rolled on, we discussed with my medical staff how best to keep me on track with the school curriculum. I was truly grateful for the support of my family, and the friends who surrounded me during that time.

My life had become a strategy game against my own body. Each game ended with victories and losses, but after each battle, both the opponent and I were changed. My scars were proof of those battles, and in the end, I was willing to wage another one because after all, those scars were evidence that I was still here. I was still alive – still breathing – still navigating my way through life. And I was still searching for normal.

Chapter Ten

I was used to the routine of packing for a stay in the hospital. But three to four months seemed like a lifetime; and this was difficult to wrap my head around. The one saving grace had been that the doctors decided I would be allowed to go home on weekends; but it made the prospect of this extended stay no less unappealing.

I packed my clothes and the portable bits of my life: my walkman to help me zone out; frames with pictures of my family and friends to give me strength; my favorite stuffed animal – a worn-out rabbit Mom had sewn for me; and a calendar to help me count down the days and help provide me with a sense of moving forward. After one more look around the house, I went over to Sparky's cage, and lifted off the top in order to pet his soft fur.

"See you later, Sparky."

"Are you ready?" Mom asked.

"Yes." I took a deep breath, and put on my coat.

Despite having done my best to follow my medical team's advice – doing all the exercises, and taking the medications – it had been to no avail. I was still being sent away. I tried to reconcile my flashbacks to early childhood with the fact that this stay would likely save my life; but it was hard to separate that knowledge from the fact that I was being ripped away from my family.

As we drove to the hospital, I tried to mentally prepare myself for this new phase of my life. I hoped ... that my body would reawaken in the spring, just as the snow-covered land that we passed would. I hoped ... the medical team and the staff would treat me better than those I had encountered during the five-week hip episode. I hoped ... my spirit had the strength to fight whatever my body threw at it. I had hoped ... that at the end of the admission, I would leave stronger than when I arrived.

As we passed through the squeaky electronic doors into the quiet lobby, an odor of cleaning fluids and other equally unpleasant hospital-related smells greeted us. The wristband they slapped on my arm felt like the brand of ownership.

A mass of new hallways and open areas led us to the ward that would soon be my Monday to Friday home. As we entered the ward, a nurse strolled over to us.

"Alison, we've been waiting for your arrival. Let's get you settled in your room."

She smiled, and led us to a room at the end of the hallway.

"The first bed is yours."

She pointed to a closet in the middle of the room.

"You can put your things in here. I'll return with the paperwork."

Dad put my suitcase on the bed; and I took off my coat in an effort to try and make myself feel at home.

"How about I hang that up for you?" Mom asked.

I looked over at the two beds, the *hospital corners* of their blankets ready to suffocate their occupants. One was occupied by a younger girl, completely-bedridden, who was listening to a hockey game. The radio drowned out the uncomfortable silence, and reminded me that there was still a world outside the hospital. Mom and I tried to make the new area my own by unpacking my personal items, and placing them around my bed.

As I opened the middle drawer of my bedside cabinet, I was faced with a blue plastic wash basin and a kidney bowl. I had been trying think about this as a process of moving into a new place – making it seem as though I was just doing a little home decorating. But those two items snapped me back to the reality that this was a hospital; this was not an adventure, and these might potentially be the longest few months in my life.

The nurse returned with a clipboard full of paperwork to complete, detailing all the specifics of my history for Mom to fill in. Dad gave me a big hug and went out to the car, while Mom helped me into my pyjamas.

"Honey, how are you doing?" she asked.

"Great." I responded, when what I wanted to say was, *Mom, I'm so tired. I don't know if I can do this.*

Mom hugged me.

"Try to have a good night. We love you, and are so proud of you."

"I love you, too." Tears collected in the corner of my eyes, but I would not let them escape.

"I'll see you tomorrow."

Then Mom walked out the door, down the hallway, and out of view.

I lay there, in a strange bed, in a strange room, in the dark, with a stranger in the next bed. No Mom, no Dad, no Cliff, no Sparky; and no friends to talk to –

just a strange place with nothing ahead of me to contemplate but these same four walls.

The fact that I couldn't get out of the bed and into my wheelchair made me completely dependant on these new people, and I didn't like that. I tried to convince myself that if I made it through this first night, then everything would be better. But each time I drifted off, a new, unfamiliar sound awoke me – the nurses talking or walking down the hallway, announcements over the intercom system, or the girl in the next bed calling for help.

Hospital nights were long, and safety was always on my mind. Security alarms throughout the various buildings would inevitably shatter the peacefulness of the night almost every second night. It seemed as if every time I finally drifted off to sleep, there was some kind of alarm or reason for our room door to be slammed loudly shut.

In a misguided attempt to occupy my overactive brain, I planned my potential escape in the case of a fire. I pinpointed how I would tie the bed sheets together and climb out the window. My limited strength, and the fact that the window might not even open at all, seemed to stop my various plans dead in their tracks. Sure the nurses had a plan, but having *my own* plan, however unrealistic it might be, made me feel a little more secure.

The next few days were a blur of tests and countless new people introducing themselves to me. Mom would spend the day with me before returning home to make supper, before she returned with Dad to visit in the evenings. I was reintroduced to the hospital's school, the one that specialized in the education of differently-abled children, while providing physiotherapy or occupational therapy. I was pleasantly surprised to find that many of the classes were being structured similarly to an arts-based program, and the fact that the classes worked around music, helped ease the transition.

Eventually the ward became my second home, and I navigated it easily. My electric wheelchair clocked in countless miles each day, and brought me a small bit of freedom. I broke the cardinal rule of Electric Wheelchairing 101 on several occasions, and drove on high speed down the hallways, gently bumping the hallway doors open with my feet. I was a racer, speeding down the tracks and squealing my tires around the corners.

Some days flew by, while others lingered, each second, minute and hour crawling by at a snail's pace. Some days my strength ebbed from of my body with each completed exercise. On those days I focused my thoughts on the coming evening visit with Mom and Dad. In fact, on many occasions it was the only thing that kept me going.

I often found myself in the main dining room clock-watching, trying to keep myself occupied until Mom and Dad arrived. I would try to distract myself with homework, music, or a television, but I constantly found myself driving back to my room window to search the parking lot for the brown sedan. I felt a twinge of excitement every time the elevator signaled a floor stop. When the elevator doors opened and strangers exited, my heart sunk every time. But the faint crunching noise my mom's plastic jacket made when she walked was the only sure-fire alert of their approach. My parents brought the smell of fresh air into my room, their hugs rejuvenated me along with

94

the promise of one day leaving this place and never returning.

After battling through each long night, I would start the morning focused on meeting my physiotherapist, Ella, at the swimming pool. I still harbored a great deal of apprehension when it came to water, but since the therapy was so important to my recovery and, ultimately, my discharge, I was determined not to let the fear take over. So taped up with plastic bandages covering my sores, I braved the deep.

The warm water lapped against my body and I had to admit, it felt good. Ella wheeled over a metal and canvas chair-on-wheels, which was my transportation down the ramp and into the pool. Despite my previous misgivings, it was clear that the water allowed me to complete the exercise more easily, and with less physical strain. After each pool exercise session, my body returned to its usual weight, and I remarked at the leadenness and fatigue I felt any time I did the exercises outside of the pool.

A few weeks into my hospitalization, my other physiotherapist, Ruby, remarked that progress on improving the function of my hands and finger joints had plateaued.

"Keep doing the exercises to prevent the function from declining any more, but I think you should start wearing a brace to maintain the progress you've made."

They were hardly the words of encouragement I'd been waiting for – mainly, that the mobility in my hands was likely to worsen, rather than improve.

The brace room gave off a wave of warmth as the oven worked its magic on the things made of plastic.

The shelves were lined with all manner of adhesives, Velcro straps and plastic sheets used for molding. Ruby drew an outline of each of my hands before cutting them out of a sheet of plastic, the sound of the scissors slicing through the hard plastic reminding me of an airplane sheering through the cold air.

"You can relax now for a bit." Ruby said, as she placed the piece of solid plastic in the oven and closed the door. "After this cools a bit, we can shape it to your wrist."

A few moments later she pulled the flexible plastic out of the oven and set it on a towel.

"Let me know if the stretch is starting to be painful."

She stretched my fingers out and pressed the warm plastic up against them. As it cooled, the plastic hardened into the shape of my small wrist. Strips of Velcro and adhesive were applied to allow me to easily open and close the brace. I knew that the brace was essential to retaining the limited amount of mobility I had, but I hated displaying to the world one more identifier of my difference.

Everyday was something of a balancing act when it came to school and therapy. And on the day when I received my brace, the balance had been lost. I returned to a music class in progress, only to find that my instructors believed that I was purposely scheduling my therapy sessions during class time – the implication being that I was deliberately attempting to shirk my academic responsibilities.

The reality was, there were only so many hours in a day. Therapy would, by necessity, occasionally overlap with my classes. I was already working on two separate curricula during the day, spending three hours in physio, with just one hour for lunch. The rest of my time during the day was spent entirely in the classroom – I wasn't sure how, exactly, amidst all those demands on my time anyone could even suggest that I wasn't holding up my end of the bargain.

So Mom and I went down to the principal's office to discuss the situation and try to find a solution. He sat tall in his chair with his hands resting on his desk. He scanned my file's contents before scowling intensely at me.

"School is important," he said to my mother. "Alison has to keep up with it. Our teachers are doing their best."

"Absolutely, but…" Mom started to say.

"Avoiding classes will not help her any," he said accusingly, closing my file.

"I was at therapy – not avoiding classes."

Anger built up inside me, and I struggled to maintain composure.

"The fact is, I'm not sure how I'm supposed to be able to complete my school assignments when *everyone else* has me scheduled with other things during my class time."

His face filled with a rosy color, I was unclear as to whether it was out of embarrassment, or anger.

"Miss Neuman, each teacher is concerned with your success. I will look into your situation."

He stood, walked to the door and opened it for us to leave, but not a word was said acknowledging what I had said.

Not a single concrete change resulted from our meeting, except that now the teacher's approached me condescendingly – as if institutional scheduling failures were somehow an indication of personal failure on my part. I was no longer a child, and I resented being treated like one. After all, in a few months I was going to be sixteen – the age where legally I was able to take responsibility for my own schooling. Obviously, I was going to complete my schooling, but the decision would be out of their hands entirely. And the idea, that the way to encourage me to keep up with my work was by treating me like an idiot, was beyond me.

During one of my clinic appointments, the stand-in doctor, Dr. Taskmaster, took a good look at my stressed out body.

"Alison, is something bothering you?"

"I can't keep up with my junior high assignments because they want me to do their hospital curriculum alongside all the therapy. I can't keep up with it all. I need to pass Grade Eight."

To my surprise, she responded with immediate concern.

"I will get that straightened out. Don't you worry – just keep on with your studies."

After that, the time I spent at the hospital school was devoted to completing my actual curriculum content. Class time was spent on my assignments only – with the option of participating in the hospital school curriculum, when I needed a break. Finally, a small modicum of control had been returned to me, and I began to feel like I could get my life back on track.

Meanwhile, I was learning how to walk again. Each week my legs grew in strength. I could go longer and farther; and the pain that usually marked my day decreased.

During one of my exams by the nurses, Dr. Taskmaster came into my room and checked my chart.

"Ease up on the blood work. How's her weight?" she asked the nurse.

"Umm. Lost ten pounds since last week," the nurse replied.

"Pain levels are still high. Let's start her on an anti-inflammatory to combat that."

The nurse scanned her notes and dropped one sheet on the ground – Dr. Taskmaster had that effect on people.

They continued a conversation *about me,* but didn't once bother to include me in it.

"May I leave after my 2 p.m. physio session?" I asked. It was a Friday, and I wanted to go home just an hour early.

For the first time, Dr. Taskmaster looked up and addressed me. She tilted her head and stood up straight.

"No. You'll stay until your last class is over. Your school needs that time with you."

Then she strode out of the room.

Despite the fact that I'd clearly demonstrated that, when left to my own devices, I was more than able to keep up with my schoolwork, everyone still presumed I was neglecting my studies. No one bothered to consult me; no one even bothered to find out how desperately I wanted to succeed at school so I could return to classes with all my friends. All I wanted was to feel as though I was a part of the decision-making process, rather than simply being ordered around.

My body began to ache from the stress. It was times like that where I was exceedingly grateful for the appearance of staff who treated the person rather than the condition.

I would have given anything that day to see our ward nurse, Sherry. The woman brought sunshine to every shift she worked. When she had free time she chose to spend it with patients, one day styling my hair and sitting with my roommate and me, or just gabbing about music and movies. Sherry gave each and every patient respect. It was on days like this, she was so sorely missed.

The weekend visits home were the highlight of my week, something I worked towards during those long stretches at the hospital. On this particular Friday the drive home seemed quicker than usual, and as we passed the park and the bridge, my body relaxed and I filled with excitement.

"Hi, Sparky," I said, spotting my sweet bunny upon opening the front door. He sprinted from the living room to the front entrance, jumping around my feet and playfully nipping them. When I sat down on the couch, he jumped up for petting. The house was filled with the voices of family, laughter, and the aroma of roast chicken.

We sat down together and watched a show from Disneyland, and I dreamt of the day we could go visit and be a part of the magic.

"Maybe one day we will be able to go to Disneyland," Mom said.

"I hope I live long enough," I said, only half joking.

"You've got all the time in the world."

On Sunday the telephone rang.

"Alison ..." Dad said, "telephone."

"Hello," I said, after reaching for the receiver, "Hey Ally, are you picking up lots of new guys?" Zinnia asked me.

"No. You?"

"At our junior high? Please. They are all so immature. Not like us."

I could feel her smiling through the laughter and jokes. Tears streamed down my face as her voice connected me to my previous life, and the memories we shared. Why the call affected me so, I wasn't sure – maybe because my time in the hospital had left me feeling like an outcast – maybe because the disease eroded my self-confidence, and made me feel insignificant. Maybe it was the fact that to date, every time I had been hospitalized I had lost pieces of my life; and I presumed there would be more casualties, amongst which would be my friends.

Her phone call made all those fears melt away.

Sundays always had me feeling stalked, knowing that the elation and freedom I was experiencing being at home, would shortly be snuffed out. Going back to the hospital was, of course, an important commitment, but it left my spirit feeling broken, battered, and tired. As anyone can attest, it's hard enough just being a teenager.

As my body was changing from that of a girl into a woman, trying to move from sick to well, I wanted to get to know who this new Alison was. All I wanted was some room to grow emotionally – room to grow – to think, and to explore. At the hospital there was no room for a young adult to find herself.

During the following weeks my body began to respond positively to the anti-inflammatory medication and exercises. I was gaining back some mobility, not enough to be able to walk any distance, but enough for me to be able to transfer from the wheelchair onto a chair or bed, and allow me to feel more independent. The cramps slowed, and as I was weaned from the meds, my stomach began to feel more relaxed. I was also losing weight, easing the strain on my legs and body, giving more energy to move around.

"Would you like to visit your junior high once a week?" Dr. Taskmaster asked me, at my next check-up.

"Yes, I would," I said

So the following week I drove myself off the ward to the hospital entrance, and waited for my ride to my junior high school. I basked in the sunshine, fresh air, and hope, before I realised that my ride had still not shown up. But rather than returning to my room in defeat, I used the payphone to call home.

Cliff answered.

"The bus didn't come to pick me up for school."

"Want me to bring you home until school starts again after lunch period?"

"If you wouldn't mind."

"I'll be there in a bit."

I hung up the receiver and excitedly drove back outside. The main road was filled with traffic, and soon Cliff's truck rounded the corner and pulled up alongside me.

"Can you step up there?" Cliff motioned to the truck's running boards.

"I think so. Let me try." My legs wobbled, but held me as I transferred over and sat in the truck. He loaded my wheelchair in the back and joined me.

Freedom!

As we drove away from the hospital, a small airplane flew overhead. Cliff looked out the window at it.

"That's one of our planes." He smiled.

"How do you like teaching flying?" I asked, watching the plane fly off into the distance.

"It's neat. The first time your students are able to go solo and get their license, it's pretty rewarding. Not to mention the fact that I get to fly every day!"

We stopped at a red light, and Cliff looked over at me.

"Alison, I met a special woman. Her name is Sandi." A gentleness and light swept across his face.

"What does she do?" I looked at him.

"She's a nurse. Maybe one day I'll bring her to meet you guys."

"I can't wait."

I grinned to myself. He was obviously a bit shy to tell us about this new woman in his life, and it made me laugh to see him blush a bit.

We continued on our way to the school, and I was filled with excitement at the prospect of re-entering the life I had left behind. But my hopes were quickly dashed; it wasn't what I remembered.

The building was the same, the teachers were the same, but I was not the same. As it had before, the distance between the reality of my everyday life, and those of my fellow students, had grown.

Before, we'd had a shared history. Now those commonalities I had worked so hard to create were

103

gone, and I felt once again like a stranger in a strange land. I was no longer a member of a student council. I had different teachers. The only thing I shared with my fellow Grade Eight students was the curriculum. Being there made me feel more isolated than I had before, and I decided not to return while I was hospitalized.

Music still brought me light in moments of darkness.

A younger volunteer at the hospital, Alec, who wore casual clothes but with sweaters that made him look sophisticated, demonstrated remarkable kindness for someone in his twenties. He played the acoustic guitar proficiently and made it sing. Alec entered the open area, and the patients gathered to hear him. For those moments, the events of the day melted away. Smiles appeared on every patient's face.

The butterflies that flew in my stomach when he came around made his visits both joyful and confusing for me. Tara had often talked to me about her various crushes on boys at school, but this was the first time I was experiencing a crush on someone other than an actor on TV. Being stuck in the house as much as I was, with a limited social circle meant there was not a huge selection of boys around to admire. And I had to admit that I found Alec handsome.

He was way too old for me, and the last thing I really wanted was to have a host of new and confusing feelings to deal with when I had so much else on my plate. But the sound of the acoustic guitar sparked my need for creativity, and Mom set up weekly lessons with Alec.

Our first lesson was in the ward's lunchroom; I took a deep breath to calm the butterflies and slow my brain down. I needed to be able to focus on the task at hand without distraction. The last thing I wanted was for him to pick up on my silly crush – especially since I was stuck in this hospital with nowhere to run to, and nowhere to hide!

Alec taught me all about the different chord structures and the different strings. Then he showed me basic chords and let me hold the guitar. It was a smaller one than others I'd seen, but it was still large for me. Pressing the strings down with my stiff, sore, fingers was a challenge, but I was eager and determined.

He showed me the chords for playing R.E.M.'s "Stand" – one of my new favorite songs. He made it seem so simple to play, and encouraged me to give it a try. According to him, all the songs were made up of these basic chords, each a combination of simple notes. Music was easier to decipher than I'd thought, and Alec told me he would teach me one note, and one chord, at a time.

Alec loaned me an acoustic guitar to take home on weekends, and I practiced on the couch until my fingertips were red and sore.

Where are those calluses when you need them?

I taped over my fingertips to allow me to play longer. And painkillers allowed me to play even longer. There was something about being able to hold the guitar on my lap, reaching my hands out to the frets, and pulling out emotions from those strings that felt freeing.

"Alison is picking up the guitar fast; she shouldn't have any trouble playing it!" Alec told my mom.

But unfortunately, in the later weeks of my stay, my fingers decided that my journey with the guitar would end. The stiffness in my joints made it difficult for me to stretch my fingers to where they needed to go, hampering my progress dramatically, and reminding me that my disease was still in control. As much as I wanted to continue playing, I realized this was a fight for which I simply didn't have the energy; I had to let it go.

This didn't stop me from keeping music front and center in my life. Sometimes we sang along to the Janet Jackson cassettes my roommate blasted. When I had worn out Debbie Gibson's *"Electric Youth,"* Tiffany's *"Hold on to an Old Friend's Hand,"* Corey Hart's *"Boy in The Box,"* or my Rock mixed tapes, I would turn up the radio. Other times, when life became frustrating and scary, my headphones and cassette player provided a song, an emotion, or a melody that allowed me to transcend to a happier, more hopeful place.

"Alison," one of the patients asked me, one day, "did you hear the news about Alec? He can't keep volunteering. He needs to get a paying job."

I was stunned. Without him, I felt like the music would die for so many of us patients there. Someone needed to try and keep that light from being extinguished. I was determined to find a way to keep Alec from leaving. So I did what I thought the best idea was for a teenager to do – I started a petition.

Computers and printers were still somewhat of a mystery to me; so on plain paper I carefully measured out the lines, and with one finger on a typewriter key at a time, I typed out the declaration. Mom and I spent the evenings visiting wards throughout the hospital, and patients of every age shared stories with us about how Alec had touched their lives. The senior citizens' eyes lit up as they spoke about his visits, and the children's parents' faces filled with joy when they spoke of how much his music had affected their child's recovery. The pages of signatures and the spoken testimonials we gathered only served to reinforce my decision to start the petition.

I delivered the brown envelope with all the support to the volunteer office, and was careful to keep its origins anonymous. As much as I wanted Alec to stay, I didn't want people to discover my crush, and sully the petitions real purpose.

A few days later, as I sat in class working on my English assignment, there was a knock at the door.

"Alison, Alec would like to talk to you," my teacher said.

Alec walked over to my desk and squatted down. He was beaming in his green cords and his favorite sweater with leather patches on the elbows. Oddly enough, I had discovered that my butterflies had vanished. I'd come to realize that I was too young, and the celebrity magic he held was not real ... he was just a man who played music. And the fact that I realized that meant I could now interact with him on a level of friendship deeper than we'd had before.

"Alison, I just heard you're responsible for the petition. I can't believe that you did all that for me," he said. "I'm going to work something out so I can stay. Thank you."

"We'd miss your music too much."

With a grateful smile, he stood up and walked out into the hallway.

Shortly after that, the day I had waited so many

months for had arrived. Today the X on my calendar was the last one I was going to mark. I sat waiting in my room as Mom had one last meeting with my social worker to ensure anything we required would be set up before we left.

When she returned to my room to help me finish packing, I noticed she was smiling oddly.

"Mom, is everything okay?"

She was beaming.

"Honey, the social worker submitted your wish to go to Disneyland. Alison, the Rainbow Society approved it. They are going to make your trip to Disneyland possible."

My eyes widened in disbelief.

"Seriously?"

"The social worker just wanted to let me know the good news."

I was ecstatic as Mom and I hugged each other. I would leave the hospital with two incredible gifts – the opportunity to fulfil my dream of going to California, and the time I needed to take advantage of that opportunity.

In fact, as I took stock of everything that had happened across those months, I realized that I'd gained much more. Up until this point, I'd never fully known who Alison was. During this time, I'd found her. She was strong, and she had a sense of humor. She loved music, was kind, and had wonderful friends and family. I'd found myself, but now I needed to find my place in the world.

Chapter Eleven

Slowly, I was beginning to feel free again. My heart felt full, as though the locks on some invisible chains that held me down had been picked open. It would take time for me to reconnect to the world outside the hospital walls, but I was going to enjoy every minute of it. My excitement at being released was bolstered, when shortly after my discharge, we met with the Rainbow Society to discuss the big trip. A bright and friendly woman in professional attire greeted us at the entrance, and reached out her hand to Mom and me.

"Hello Alison and Violet. I'm Victoria, and this is Piper. Are you ready to plan your family's trip?"

"Thank you so much." I worked hard to hold back my tears.

"You're welcome," she said with a warm smile.

I tried to absorb the trip schedule and details during the meeting – but it was almost too much. This was all actually happening. It was real now.

Because neither Dad nor Cliff would be able to go with us due to their work schedules, my Aunt Myrtle from British Columbia would be able to join us. In the days before the trip, time seemed to slow to a crawl. Little activities, like purchasing American currency and getting our packing ready, help remind us of the adventure to come, and Myrtle's arrival kept me from spending all my time counting the minutes before our departure.

The morning of our escape, the window revealed a cold and snowy October morning; the forecast for Los Angeles – even with some rain – looked to be balmy by Edmonton standards. With our coats and bags ready, and my medication at full strength, we climbed into our car for the long drive to the airport. Once there, we positioned ourselves at our airline's check-in line.

Dad smiled at us as we readied ourselves.

"See you later, girlies. Have good trip."

He gave me a big hug, and as he moved on to Mom, a tear collected in my eye at the fact that Dad and Cliff would miss our adventure. But there was no time to wallow as I was quickly whisked away in a slim, uncomfortable wheelchair provided by the airline. I watched them tag my comfortable wheelchair and send it onto the airplane as we made our way to the gate

We were escorted onto the pedway by a pretty flight attendant who pointed to the airplane outside the window.

"That's the aircraft we're flying on to Los Angeles."

"Can I take a picture? I promised my brother. He loves to fly."

"Sure!"

Inside the plane, the attendant pulled the sides off of the wheelchair and pushed me easily between the rows of seats before helping me to settle in to my seat. Mom sat next to me and Aunt Myrtle next to the isle.

My heart filled with excitement as the engines geared up to full power and we started down the runway. As the airplane lifted off the ground, and the force pressed my back into my seat, I felt like every piece of emotional baggage I'd ever had, had been left on the Edmonton tarmac. Within four short hours, we touched down on the LAX runway, greeted by a cloudy, but warm day.

We made our way to the hotel in a shuttle, passing by Disneyland, surrounded by its topiaries trees shaped like characters from all the beloved movies. My window-side cot in the hotel afforded a captivating view of blue sky dotted with small white fluffy clouds at each sunrise and sunset. At least, it did when the smog wasn't too bad. The next day started with breakfast at a restaurant conveniently located a few steps from our hotel. It was hard not to rush and say, "Come on, come on, let's go."

Warm weather, and the short distance from the hotel, allowed us to be able to walk to Disneyland. So as Mom pushed me past the flower-lined hotels we basked in the glow of being able to wear spring coats in October. And suddenly, we were there – Disneyland.

As we entered the front gate, the sight of the magnificent castle caused tears to well up in my eyes. My heartbeat quickened. There is, without a doubt, something magical about that place – regardless of your age. But more than that, I'd never thought this would become a reality. At many times, I didn't think I'd even live long enough to contemplate this journey.

So armed with my new camera – an early birthday present from Cliff – I snapped my way through a memory-filled adventure I'd dreamt about since I'd first heard of the *magical kingdom* as a small child. The day was marred only slightly by the back pain that prevented me from going on the rides. But ultimately, the outside world and all the stress, was behind me. I tried to soak everything in like a sponge. I took account of every minute, and every hour that passed, grateful for every moment of freedom.

The next day we took a cab to Universal Studios – yet another dream destination for me. Even as we passed the famous Hollywood sign in the distance, I still couldn't quite fathom that I was seeing it firsthand. We were actually in the same place where all movies and television shows were made – shows that had sparked my imagination and fought back against the loneliness of so many hospital stays.

We had just begun to tour the vast grounds when we walked past a building with a sign reading:

Make Your Own Music Videos

I stopped dead in my tracks, and went inside to check out the prices.

"Honey, if you want to – go for it!"

"You sure? It might take a while."

"We're in no hurry. We're here to have fun."

"Get to your video, young lady!" Aunt Myrtle instructed me, smiling

It was too good an opportunity to miss. I could live out my singing dream, and at Universal Studios, no less!

The surfer dude behind the counter greeted me cheerfully.

"First you'll lay down a vocal track, and then we'll totally make a video."

He led us into a recording studio whose walls were covered in pointed foam. Before me, stood a music stand adjusted to my height, my lyric sheet and a set of headphones. Mom slid the large headphones on my head and they promptly slipped right off.

"They're being stubborn! They don't want to stay on your head." We both laughed and fiddled with them until they cooperated.

Mom left the room while I prepared myself mentally to sing Debbie Gibson's "*Lost in Your Eyes*." I'd sung it at home countless times, but I wasn't sure that my voice was in prime condition. As the track started to play, I followed the female voice in my headphones, and sang along once to practice.

"Alright, I'm going to record you this time."

Despite all my best efforts, my voice betrayed me –squeaking and cracking on some of the high notes. But there was no *do-over,* and soon Surfer Dude entered the room again and set a keyboard in front of me.

"Now let's film that video." He closed the door and the track played as I pretended to play the keyboard and sing along. This was the fun part, and I played it up completely.

When I was done, I found Mom and Aunt Myrtle out in the main foyer watching the engineer mix the vocal track and video. They'd been able to watch the whole thing on the television.

"You were great!" Mom said as she wheeled me out. It was fun to feel like a rock star, even if it was just for a short while.

The magic of the movies and television was in abundance throughout Universal Studios. Behind a set

113

of red ropes I spotted a familiar black sports car that just happened to be having a conversation with some girls. I immediately recognised it as KITT from *Knight Rider*. Many an evening we had gathered in the living room to watch David Hasslehoff's adventures with this amazing car, and there KITT was, right in front of me! And not only that, it was having an interactive conversation with these girls. Despite my best efforts I couldn't find evidence of a single camera or recording device anywhere that might be used to feed information to whoever might be behind that unmistakable voice.

Ongoing back pain prevented me from being able to go on the tram tour, but I refused to allow Aunt Myrtle to miss out. So as she went on the tour, Mom and I stayed on the grounds sitting in the sunshine, and simply enjoying our lunch against the exciting backdrop. Back pain or not, it was the trip of a lifetime; and being able to forget about the pressure of schedules and doctors' visits was, in itself, an incredible vacation for us both.

The next day we headed to the docks for a cruise to Catalina Island. The water stretched out before me, as far as the eyes could see. The sound of the waves splashing up against the boat reminded me how far away from the prairies we really were. Two tall, strong crewmen – one very handsome, indeed – gently lifted my wheelchair onto the boat deck. We found a seat inside, next to a window. Once out at sea I began to see small grey fins peering out above the water's surface.

"Mom, are those really dolphins?"

"I think so," Mom said.

Then a dolphin jumped out of the water, confirming its presence. Soon two dolphins were gracefully frolicking amongst the waves, guiding us to our destination.

Reaching Catalina Island, I was finally able to check off one last item on my California *to-do* list; the beach, the white sand, and the ocean were calling me. Dozens of sun worshippers sat on the beach, reading and tanning. To them, it must have seemed commonplace, but I had never seen the ocean that close before, other than on the airplane. I'm sure my smile almost touched my ears when I saw the beach and ocean that close-up.

"Mom, can we take off my shoes so I can feel the sand and water between my toes?"

"We'll do our best!" Mom replied as she moved to push my wheelchair into the sand. But instead of gliding on top of it, it got completely stuck. Yet again, we found ourselves in need of a tow-truck, and the three of us convulsed into giggles. But this time we had the strength of two women, and between Mom and Aunt Myrtle we were able to make our way over to the water's edge. The ocean mist caressed my face, and the warm sand squished between my toes. I banked that sensory experience in my memory bank where it has remained with me ever since.

Our last day in Anaheim came far too quickly. While I missed my family and friends, for a short time all my troubles melted away, and being there had made me feel like I could handle whatever challenges the future held in store. But I felt like that feeling would stay with me; my batteries were recharged, and my spirit was ready to continue the battle.

At the airport, an airline attendant approached us. "We have a family wishing to travel together. Would it be possible to move you to first class?"

Mom looked at all of us for approval.

"I guess so."

While most people would jump at the chance for an upgrade, being a newbie flyer and being seated apart from my family, made me a bit nervous. A business man was seated next to me, so I tried to follow his lead on how the whole *first class* thing worked. After I had looked through the complimentary newspaper, the flight attendant came down the isle with silver trays holding steaming hot white cloths. I copied my neighbor, wiping my hands with the cloth, trying to look as though I'd done this a million times before.

As I turned to talk to Mom, who was seated behind me, the man addressed Mom.

"How about we trade seats, and you can sit with your daughter?"

We gratefully accepted, and once Mom was seated next to me, we were truly able to enjoy the business class experience in all its glory. We were brought a platter of food that looked like it had come from a real restaurant, rather than from the tiny food cabinets that stored the economy class dinners. And soon after that, they came with another tray of food.

"I thought that was the meal, Mom!"

"Me, too, honey. Me, too" Mom and I laughed. We could get used to first class in a hurry.

As we approached Edmonton, the multi-colored lights of the city reflected my excitement to be home. The trip had been more than a vacation; it was a break from all the stress and havoc that my health wreaked on my life.

When we exited the double doors from customs, Dad stood waiting, and a huge smile spread across his face. As he hugged me close, I found comfort in the familiarity of home. And I found even greater comfort in the realization that dreams do come true.

Chapter Twelve

"Alison, tonight I'm bringing Sandi over so all of you can meet her. Try not to scare her away," Cliff said, smiling.

"I'm looking forward to meeting her!" I answered, and I'd meant it.

All my life I had dreamed of having a sister; the thought that maybe one day, Cliff would find someone that might fit the bill, even as an in-law, had always been in the back of my mind. And as soon as the prospect of Sandi appeared, I was consumed by that possibility –completely ignoring the fact that this meant my brother might have found someone special.

The creak of our backdoor signaled their arrival, and Cliff and Sandi walked into our dining area. Sandi had dark short hair, and her slim figure was flattered by her blue jeans and sweater. She was neatly accessorised and I'd never seen anyone look so good wearing such casual clothes.

"Mom, Dad, Alison, this is Sandi." Cliff introduced her as Sandi shook our hands.

Her blue eyes sparkled as she greeted me.

"Hi, Alison."

"Sandi, it's a pleasure to meet you."

As we sat at the dining table chatting, I observed Cliff and Sandi occasionally rubbing on one another's arms or holding hands; it was clear this was no puppy love.

"Sandi's a nurse," Cliff said.

"I was once, too," Mom added.

At that point the conversation moved into more adult territory, and I soon found myself left out. So I snuck off into the living room to watch *Star Trek: The Next Generation* on television. Sandi soon joined me, sitting down on the floor right next to me.

"What do you think of this batch of characters?" she asked.

"They're good, but I liked the first series better."

"Yeah. I think the first series was better, too."

I'd been pleasantly surprised to find her interested in the show, and it proved to be the opening we needed. We soon found we shared many interests from music to movies, and the fact that she was a nurse also meant she had a clear understanding of just how different my life was from other kids. We talked about her family and her dog, and how we shared a love of teasing Cliff about the carpentry shows he loved to watch. Hours had passed and it still felt too soon when Cliff took her home. I couldn't wait to see her again.

The increasing number of bouts I'd had with back pain, and the more time I spent in sitting, meant that I'd lost a lot of strength in my legs. As a result, I found myself unable to get up out of my wheelchair without help. The freedom of movement the chair had given me had also left me feeling helpless. I knew that the only way to combat this was to get my muscles and joints moving. I needed to walk again.

When I could no longer stand the frustration and helplessness, I decided to park my wheelchair at the end of our small kitchen. My goal was to get to the other end of the kitchen without stopping and without anyone helping me. Using a walker my family had borrowed for me, I placed my feet on the cream-colored tiled floor and rocked myself until I was in a standing position. I leaned on the walker with my arms, while my legs tried to remember how to stand. My muscles fought my brain, and after a few minutes of just standing there, I needed to sit down and call it a day. I knew one day I'd be able to walk to the end of the kitchen with the walker, but in the meantime, it was a very slow, painful, and frustrating process.

First, just being able to stand up was an accomplishment – then, taking one or two steps with the aid of the walker. Each step I took was confronted by the strong deterrent of pain and my lack of muscle strength. My body would only let me push it so far. Sometimes it was a week or a month before I made any significant progress. But eventually I was able to take a few steps on my own, minus the walker.

What an accomplishment to feel like a small child just starting out and being able to take my first steps. Even though I could not go very far, the sense of security and independence those tiny strides gave me was priceless.

Having been out of hospital for some time, I'd been eager to rekindle the relationships with my friends and regain those elements of my social life that'd I'd lost during my tenure there. Once a week, Grace and her mom, Ivy, came over and we drank tea and played cards or board games – *Team Daughter* against *Team Mom*. This week's game was *Pictionary*. Grace's mom could replicate nearly any object with extreme precision, but even if Grace and I were not particularly talented artists, we were on the same wavelength.

120

Grace drew a cow and a glass.

"Milkshake," I said.

Grace smiled, and laughed.

"Yep!"

"No way, let's see," her Mom said incredulously as we looked over to see her still life drawing of a milk jug and a blender. It reminded me that despite the distance, Grace and I still had that connection we'd always had.

Grace had never been thrown off by my wheelchair and never hesitated to come out for a walk – well, *push* –with me, go for coffee, and do whatever other things typical sixteen-year-olds do. We'd go to the mall to browse for fashions, music, or just through the teen magazines.

I had made the decision after my hospitalization not to return to the regular junior high school that Grace and Tara attended. I knew I wouldn't be able to run for council, and the stress I'd experienced being ripped out of my routine proved too much for me to handle. I wasn't eager to repeat that experience should I be required to have yet another lengthy hospital stay. I opted instead to finish my diploma through distance education. I had worried that it might hinder my social life, but I was happy to discover that it didn't. As we all matured and developed our own interests, it became clearer that we didn't need to be in the same building to be able to relate.

One day while we were playing cards, we got to talking about my love of music and singing.

"Alison," Grace said, "maybe we should sing together. You know, as a duo."

I hadn't really known she'd been that interested in singing before, so I was pleasantly surprised by her suggestion, and readily agreed. We decided to call ourselves the *"Electric Knights,"* naming ourselves after the last names of some boys we liked. Then we set out selecting the perfect song – one we both liked and could learn to perform together – *"Flash Dance,"* by Irene Cara.

We devoted all of our after school time together practicing and harmonizing until we knew it inside and out. We'd perfected our version of the song, and it seemed as good a time as any to take it to the next level.

"There's a contest coming up at a local mall. Want to enter?" I asked.

"The *Electric Knights* are ready for their debut," she said.

So every day, after Grace was out of school, we practiced in the privacy of my bedroom with my backing track. We purchased two skirt ensembles, one pink and one purple, which Mom embellished with gold chains, lightening bolts made of sequins.

When the big day arrived, we went to our local mall in our matching dresses and waited by the stage for our turn. I'd taken some strong meds to enable me to get out of my wheelchair just long enough to stand up on the stage and complete the song. I figured that to perform the song I really needed to be standing. It also gave me better breath control. Inside I wanted to be the best I could for Grace. I was desperate not to forget any words or do anything that might jeopardize her chances of advancing in the competition. I didn't want her *different friend* to be the reason she didn't succeed.

We heard our names, and Grace grabbed my hand and helped me get up on the stage. There I stood, my legs locked to keep me upright, trying to catch my breath from the exertion of climbing the three small steps. As shoppers rushed back and forth, the background music began to play. The event coordinators sat by the front of the stage and mall-goers stood around watching. We held our microphones up and made our way seamlessly through each verse and chorus. At a certain point, we both looked at each other and realised we were actually enjoying ourselves. And while we didn't win, the value of that time on stage wasn't lost on either of us.

Our next performance, the following year, was at a local talent show, where I had once danced with other students. We kicked our rehearsal regiment back into gear, practicing daily. This time we'd chosen a new song, "*Like We Never Had a Broken Heart*," by Trisha Yearwood. We'd worked hard to harmonize our voices, and to take everything we'd learned from our first experience and apply it to this performance. And this time, the work had paid off; when we received our performance certificates, we were informed that we'd gotten a high enough mark to move on to the city finals, to be held late spring.

So we added another song to our portfolio – "*A Whole New World*." We'd decided to use some chairs as props, which allowed me to sit while singing. Sitting took the edge off my pain; this allowed me to focus on the experience and on controlling my voice. And lo and behold, at the end of the day we'd garnered ourselves second place at the municipal level, and took home a silver medallion each. Barring a first place finish – the entire process couldn't have gone better.

But the following week, during one of our game sessions, Grace turned to face me, and stopped dealing the cards.

"Alison, can we go solo – for now, anyway? I just don't want to let you down if I forget a word."

"You never let me down, but if that's what you want, we can do that."

"Still best buddies forever though?" Grace reached out her hand to shake mine.

"Friends forever." I shook her hand.

While I tried not to let it show, my heart sunk in my chest. After all this time singing together, after all our successes it was over. Just like that. I knew she felt the same kind of pressure as I did – working with a partner always meant you had someone else depending on you. But this had been more than just a chance to sing. It had been a chance to fit in. It had given me the sense of belonging that I so desperately craved, and now it was gone.

One day, while we were grocery shopping at the mall, I noticed two new employees were working at my favorite music store. Actually, I'm not sure if they had been there all along, but it was only then that Nicole and I noticed them. Not knowing the boys real names, we decided to give them nicknames. Since we both loved the show *Perfect Strangers,* I decide to call the one with long black hair and a bright smile Larry, and Nicole gave the shorter one with curly hair the name Balki—we soon found out that they resembled their nicknames in appearance only.

One day Larry was taking the money for a cassette tape I was buying and before I could stop myself, I opened my mouth and started to speak.

"I was wondering if you would tell me your name?" I asked.

Did I just ask that out loud? Oh no.

I felt my face flush.

"Why?" He looked up at me.

"My friend and I were trying to figure out your names. We gave you nicknames, but I'm sure they're not even close."

"What names did you give us?" he asked as he put my cassette into a bag.

"Larry and Balki." His eyes sparkled as a smile lit up his face.

"I'm the manager," he said pointing to the business cards. "You can take one. What's your name?"

"Alison."

I left the store and looked at the card. *Matthew Smith – Manager.*

Matthew suited him much better.

Mom and I usually went to the mall around three or four times a week, just to have an outing that got us out of the house and get a little exercise walking. Any time Matthew saw us in our wandering he'd come over, or if I was outside the store he would wave us in to come in to talk. I don't know exactly when it happened, but at some point I started to feel different about those talks. I was starting to feel a connection with him, one that induced those tell-tale butterflies.

"My band played a gig last night," he mentioned to me casually one day.

"Do you sing?"

"I sing and write."

I was starting to like everything about him: his
smile; his knowledge of music; and his acceptance of
my world. He seemed to look beyond my disease, my
wheelchair – to find the real girl behind it all.

"So does your disease affect your woman things?"
he suddenly asked very matter-of-factly.

"No, everything is fine."

I could feel myself blushing as the realization of
what he had just asked me sank in. Now if it had been
anyone else who had asked me that, I might have had
an issue, but despite the growing rosiness of my
cheeks, I still felt comfortable discussing it with him.
He then began to tell me about his girlfriend, and how
she too was dealing with a serious health issue; I knew
that he must be a very special man who could look past
all that. I was struck by a momentary sadness that a
man with such maturity was already taken, but it
quickly passed; I just loved having him as a part of my
life, no matter how small. I couldn't help but hope that
one day that I would be lucky enough to be able to find
a man – someone like Matthew – who could look past
my body, my disease, and love me for the soul and
heart hidden beneath.

I didn't see Matthew much after that day, our
routines had just changed. But some years later, our
paths crossed once again. We had both moved on to
new people and relationships, but found we could still
share almost anything with one another. Before we
knew it we had been talking for over an hour. He
confided in me that of all the girls he had met, he had
never forgotten me. But of course, at the time, I was
far too young, and not in any space for a mature
relationship. And of course, that many years later my
own feelings for him had changed, but I remained

grateful that he was the first man who offered me that glimpse at someone who would value *all* the elements of my being, regardless of what others thought.

Cliff's work schedule over the last months had become increasingly demanding, so between that and spending time with Sandi, the opportunities to visit were rare. So when he was home I always took advantage of the opportunity. One evening, Cliff and I met in the bedroom hallway, when he turned to me.

"Check this out."

I took the piece of paper from his hand, unfolding it. The receipt was for a diamond ring setting.

"Is this for an engagement ring?"

"I'm going to take Sandi to Jasper in two weeks and ask her," he said, a huge grin spreading across his face.

My heart skipped a beat. I realised that this was it – he had found his special woman. But I realised – more selfishly – that I was finally going to get that sister I had always wanted, and I was ecstatic.

"That's wonderful, Cliff!"

"Alison, don't tell anyone yet, please."

"I won't," though I secretly wondered how I would ever manage to keep such an enormous secret to myself.

That weekend, as Cliff took my future sister-in-law to the mountains I kept one eye on the clock. I was praying she said *yes*, since we all thought she was a very special woman. The weekend finally over, the back door opened, and in came Cliff and Sandi. Cliff was carrying a bottle of champagne in one hand, and was holding Sandi's with the other. They sat down on our couch, and we all joined them in the living room.

"Well, congratulate us," Cliff said.

"Why?" Dad asked.

"We're engaged!" Cliff lifted up Sandi's hand so we could see the ring. Both of them were absolutely beaming.

We each took turns hugging them as Sandi proudly held out her hand, and showed us the ring. I had seen Cliff happy before, but I had never seen him like this. It made me realize how exciting real love must be, and made me look all the more forward to experiencing it one day.

Cliff looked at Mom and Dad.

"You really didn't know?"

"No, why? Should we have?" Dad asked.

"I told Alison. I was sure she would slip!"

"You asked me not to," I said.

He smiled at me.

Cliff and Sandi decided to get married in Jasper, Alberta – a special place for them both. Traveling was never simple for me, always involving complicated packing with my meds and supplies, but I was excited to go. Grace and I drove down halfway with Uncle Ingmar, and the other way with Dad. With our Walkmen playing music, and the excitement of my first wedding, the drive seemed more fun than arduous.

The mountains greeted us at the park gate, and we made our way to the inn where our cabin had been reserved. Grace sat on the floor of the loft with her legs hanging down, and swinging against the railing overlooking the living room. Staying up in the loft meant that I'd have to be on constant medication in order to make it up and down the stairs, but I figured it was well worth it for the adventure of having our own space.

It was pouring outside, but Grace and I ventured across the parking lot to pick up some nachos to eat in the room. We sat under the cover of the balcony eating nachos. As we watched the raindrops collect into puddles, I dreamt about having Sandi in our family.

The day before, Sandi had approached me at a gathering at their house.

"Alison and Grace, we were wondering if you would set up the candles on the front table of the church for us?"

"Yes," Grace said.

"Absolutely," I echoed.

"And Alison," Cliff added, "we would like you to do a reading at our wedding. Will you?"

"I would be honored," I said.

The passage I was reading was from Corinthians. There were words in the passage I was unsure of, and at the rehearsal I replaced all those words with "*whatever*," and got a few laughs. But every spare minute I had, I rehearsed the piece over and over until the words were etched in my memory, and I could pronounce them effortlessly.

And then, the day had arrived.

"Alison, Grace, let's go to the church to set up the table," Dad said, and we excitedly made our way over to the venue.

The church was filled with the aroma of fresh orchids lining the pews. We set two white candles ensconced in small gold candleholders on either end of the main altar. In the middle was a candle with both Cliff and Sandi's names on it. Once we had finished setting it all up, we sat down in the pews.

Cliff stood at the front of the church in a black tuxedo. Sandi was breathtaking as she walked down the aisle. Her white satin princess dress was adorned with lace and crystals; and a long white train matched her dress and shoes. She was holding a bouquet of white orchids with pink and yellow flowers throughout. As she walked passed where we were sitting, she winked at me.

My heart filled with joy as the ceremony proceeded and the moment where they'd announce her officially joining of our family approached. On cue, I stood by the podium and looked at the first pew where Cliff and Sandi were sitting.

Sandi looked at me and smiled, as the two of them clutched each other's hands tightly. I was grateful for the extra time I'd expended practicing the pronunciation of the words in the reading and was happy to have been able to contribute to their special day.

After all our readings, Cliff and Sandi lit their candle and signed the registry. Then it came, the words we'd been waiting for – "Mr and Mrs Cliff Neuman."

We all cheered and clapped, and tears filled my eyes to witness such happiness.

The photos outside were set against the gorgeous backdrop of the mountains, and waiting in front of the church for Cliff and Sandi, was a carriage decorated in aquamarine pompoms and white wedding bells. A white horse with brown spots waited patiently to take them to their reception.

It was the kind of evening everyone dreams of – wonderful food, new family members embracing one another, and dancing and celebrating into the early hours of the morning. I was captivated by it all, especially watching Cliff and Sandi's first dance.

I hoped one day to have a love like that for myself. For this weekend, life was full of so much joy and excitement for our family and the future ahead.

Chapter Thirteen

A professional performance choir was holding auditions, and since my performance opportunities with Grace had ended, the idea really piqued my interest; I decided to take a shot at it. I feared that the presence of my wheelchair as an indicator of a physical disability would hurt my chances of success, so I took extra medication and kept it hidden from view in our car's trunk.

Grace was joining me, and we sat together at the audition watching the other girls as they entered the music room, one at a time. Finally I was called in and introduced to the choir director, a tall, slim woman, who was dressed in business attire.

Please don't blow this.

She had me sing a bit, answer a few questions, and then marked something down on a sheet of paper. I stood, nervously waiting for her to say something.

"Alison, you are invited to join our choir. Rehearsals are Thursday evenings in this room. See you Thursday."

I did it.

The shot of adrenalin that came from my victory pushed any pain from my body, and I worked hard to maintain my composure and walk calmly out of the room.

Grace entered immediately after me, and when she came out with a huge smile on her face, we knew we'd both made it. Even though we'd decided to go *solo*, neither of us could conceal the fact that we were thrilled to have this opportunity to sing together; neither of us would be alone in this new venture.

The practices took place once a week for an hour and a half. Learning to sing first soprano was a challenge, but I was in my element. Even though the audition phase had long since passed, I still felt nervous about how I might appear to other choir members. We were fortunate that there was parking close by, so my need to walk was limited. But I still tried to manage my drink intake in the afternoon to avoid having to take trips to the washroom. But I was paying a price to try and keep up the impression of *normalcy*. For each choir practice where I avoided using my wheelchair, I spent the next day in intense pain, my mobility even more reduced than usual.

All new members were required to get a new performance dress that matched with the rest of the choir. Our parents were provided fabric to create the robes and patterns to sew us the new dresses. As part of my participation, we were required to do many of the fundraising activities typical to these groups – selling chocolate-covered almonds, mints and the like. My mom pushed me around the neighborhood, rang the doorbells, and when the occupant came to the door I gave my best pitch. As a result of having those almonds in the house, I found my waistline began to expand a little bit.

My time with the choir gave me the performance opportunities I had so craved. The biggest thrill came when it was announced that we would perform at the Jubilee Auditorium, where countless professional musicians and recording artists had also performed.

On the day of the performance we all gathered by the *artists entrance* before being led to the dressing rooms. They were just as I had always dreamt they would be –massive mirrors were lined with bright light bulbs, just like in the movies. My dream of performing at the same level as professionals was being realised, and I soaked it in.

We were escorted to the back of the massive wooden stage where we waited quietly for the choir in front of us to finish. After their exit, we walked out in order onto the risers. We were cradled on either side by the massive curtains, and bright lights shone on us as we waited for our cues.

I was on the first set of risers and I needed a hand from a fellow choir member to steady myself when stepping up. I reminded myself to focus on the choir director and ignore the audience, which was easily done since the stage lights were so hot and bright I couldn't see anything past the stage.

Wow, I'm actually here. Soak it in, girl!

Our voices carried beautifully across the massive theatre, and we performed flawlessly. It was so exhilarating, yet it was over so quickly I hardly even felt we'd begun. And all the hours we'd dedicated to perfecting our pieces paid off.

At the next practice our director announced:

"Our choir has been selected to be a part of a special television broadcast for Christmas. On Saturday, you'll all need to come to the studio where the special will be recorded. Make sure you wear lots of make-up to look good on camera."

So there I was that next week. At a television studio, in full dress, wearing exaggerated make-up to ensure I'd look good on screen. We were led to a set decorated with Christmas trees and risers, and took our place. Under the hot lights, waiting for the film crew to reset between each song, my legs began to burn as they locked into a straight position.

Please let me able to move when we're done shooting.

My body started to overheat, and my cheeks burned with redness. Some of the girls sat down on the risers, trying to beat the heat. As much as I was desperate to rest for a spell, I refused to jeopardize the illusion I'd created for fellow choir members that I was completely normal.

If I sit down, I'll never get back up again.

Mercifully the shoot ended before I found myself on the verge of passing out. I'd carved a notch out on my achievement belt, and there was soon more to come.

At our next choir practice, we were presented with yet another incredible opportunity.

"Girls, we sent in an audition tape to sing for Disneyland's Magic Music Day in Los Angeles, California," the director informed us. We could hardly imagine her next words:

"Our year-end trip will be to perform at Disneyland."

The room erupted in cheers, myself included, as I thought about the magical place The Rainbow Society had sent us to just a few years prior. Joy leapt through my body like electricity as I thought about all the Disney movies I had grown up with and how much I loved them. To be able to participate in a performance associated with Disney left me speechless. And then reality hit me.

In a heartbeat the all too familiar lump appeared in my stomach when I thought about all the barriers that might make traveling to California impossible. Our family did not have much extra income, and the fact was that despite the façade of health I'd presented to my fellow choir members, my mom would have to travel with me to help me with basic activities. Hiding my disability for a couple of hours was one thing – keeping it hidden for days was quite another.

As the room emptied of excited girls chattering about going to California, I waited behind to speak to the director. I approached her as she picked her sheet music up from the stand, and placed it in her portfolio.

"I'm sorry. I don't think I can join the choir in L.A. With my health, I need my Mom to help me, and expense-wise, we just can't afford it." I tried too hard to hide the disappointment in my voice.

She stopped what she was doing, and turned towards me, smiling.

"Alison, your mom can travel with us as one of our chaperones. You have been fundraising like crazy; we'll work something out."

She was as good as her word. In talking with my mom, the director had learned of my disability. Watching the conversation unfold, I had grown fearful that I'd be kicked out – kicked out first, because I was different, but second, and more importantly, because I had not been entirely truthful with the director from the outset.

But rather than showing me the door, she leaned down to where I was sitting, putting one arm around me.

"Alison," she said, "your singing ability earned your spot in the choir. Not your mobility."

It was a relief to no longer be hiding my wheelchair, and even better; it meant that I could save my strength for the performances.

So, with Mom in tow, we soon found ourselves at LAX once again. As we exited customs, we saw a woman beckoning us with a sign reading:

"Columbian Girl Choir"

welcoming us. We boarded a giant tour bus, and were whisked off to the massive hotel near Disneyland that would be our home for the next several days.

The performance was scheduled to take place in the courtyard of the Disneyland hotel. We took our place on risers that had been set up on a floating deck surrounded by the balconies of hotel rooms. Hundreds of guests stood on their balconies and watched us perform for them. That sense of magic I'd felt the last time I'd been in Disneyland had returned – we all felt it. As I sung my heart out, I felt my spirit soar.

The performance over, we were afforded the privilege of attending a workshop at Disneyland by the man who handled the hiring of actors and singers. As I sat alongside other choir members in the backstage of the park, I couldn't help feel a bit intimidated to be in his company.

"First, let's relax with an activity." He stood at the front of the room and demonstrated a pattern where we pointed first to the head, then shoulders, then knees, toes, eyes, ears, mouth, and nose.

"Cue the music," He nodded at a piano player.

As we repeated the pattern to the music, the melody began to quicken. Soon it was nearly impossible to keep up, and the room dissolved into laughter. And with that, our nerves dissipated. As the workshop went on, he provided us with invaluable tips and insight to help further us in our careers. And he left us with this:

"Keep your dreams close to your heart. Write down your goals and stick them where you can see them everyday. Maybe one day I'll see you in our auditions."

I topped off what had already been an incredible year with something I'd been anticipating for years – turning eighteen.

While many of my friends were excited to reach this milestone because it meant they could drink and go to the bar, I was waiting for this day to come because it finally meant that I could say *no* to my doctors. I would be the one who either gave or withdrew consent for any tests or procedures. I was the one who would determine whether a course of treatment would be pursued or not.

I celebrated the day by going out for an afternoon drink at a local restaurant with Mom, Grace and Ivy. Selecting that first alcoholic beverage from the menu was a challenge – so I chose something that held some recognition for me, a creamsicle. But after a few sips, it lost its charm. I just didn't like the taste of liquor – but it was a rite of passage; I could order it, and I could get into a bar. The fact that singers often played in bars was not lost on me, so I recognized that it might be important to me at some time in the future.

That time arrived quicker than I'd imagined. Trying to build my singing career and gain experience, I sent in a two-song demo to a radio-sponsored contest. The demos were judged by a panel, the finalists to perform at a local bar – and I was one of those chosen few. Adding to my excitement was the fact that I would be singing with a real band, not the pre-recorded backing tracks I was accustomed to. I worked tirelessly, adopting a rigid routine practicing my phrasing and breathing, completing vocal warm-ups, and, of course taking medication.

On the night of the competition finals, I checked in to discover that not only was I the only contestant who had not competed in this particular contest before, but I was also the youngest. Mom and I found a place to sit in view of the judges' table and stage. Butterflies grew in my stomach as I watched the band set-up. As excited as I was to perform with them, none of us had been given rehearsal time with them – a situation I found nerve-wracking, to say the least.

When my turn came on the stage I nodded to the band to start playing.

Smile. Look confident. You've done this before

I was surprised by how loud the music was – hearing myself became a real challenge. But the band followed my lead, and soon the first song was over. I took a moment in between the two songs to say a word.

"I would like to dedicate this song to my Mom."

The judges smiled, and I beamed at Mom, who smiled back at me, and shyly lowered her head for a moment before I began to sing.

The performance had felt like a real jam session, and it was the closest that I had come so far, to being a real singer. The confidence I gained after each performance only served to fuel my passion more – and this had been no exception.

Many of the performers had their friends and family members at the bar rooting for them and showing support. Mom and Dad had loudly indicated their support for me too – though after seeing me perform Dad returned to the car. In typical *dad* fashion, he found it too loud and "not his style."

Being new to singing with a live band, I knew I wasn't a contender to win the contest. But it didn't matter, the experience had been invaluable, and as we were leaving, one of the judges, a local recording artist, approached me.

"Alison, thanks for coming and sharing your gift with us. We have jams once a week – you should come and join us sometime. I haven't seen you around the scene, are you new?"

"I'm just starting out."

"Well, keep at it. We'll see you around."

I knew how tough the arts scene could be. There was always someone waiting to tear you down, but he'd taken the time to build me up.

Chapter Fourteen

For our choir trip at the end of year two, they'd chartered a bus to drive us to Seattle, Washington. The bus trips gave me a real taste of what it was like to live the life of a performer. Criss-crossing from town to town, playing gigs in remote cities before getting back on that bus and heading to the next town. Every morning was a new city. I welcomed the opportunity to have a little taste of the *real* life of a singer on the road.

Our performance roster was incredibly varied. One day we were singing for the passengers boarding the *Spirit of Puget Sound* dinner cruise, after which we were able to enjoy the cruise ourselves. The cruise presented my first glimpse at the world of dinner theatre, as the waiters sung and danced in between serving the guests their meals.

Another stop along the highway found us in the recreation room of a Seattle continuing care centre, with residents arriving via walkers, canes, and wheelchairs to stake out their spots for our performance. Grace and I had included an a cappella version of *"The Greatest Man I Never Knew."* As I looked out on the aging crowd to sing the song that spoke of the relationship between a daughter and her father, I couldn't help but think of my own dad. As we finished, the residents sat quietly, many of them with their eyes welling.

141

When the show was over, an elderly resident in a floral dress wheeled herself over to us and reached out her hand to shake ours.

"Thank you for coming, and for singing that song. It reminds me of my dad."

"Thanks for having us. It reminds me of my dad, too."

"Now ya'll go and have some ice cream sundaes."

A smile spread across her face as she pointed to the make-shift sundae bar the staff had prepared for us. Even though these might not have been the grandest stages we encountered on our tour, there was no question these stops were amongst the most meaningful.

The touring also afforded us the benefit of being able to travel as a sightseer as well; and Mom, Grace, and I took full advantage of any spare time we had. So of course, the Space Needle was a *must-see*. As we drove around the winding concrete pillars that shape Seattle's skyline, the Needle remained in clear view. It towered over us, and became increasingly daunting as we approached its location. Soon we arrived and headed towards the ticket window.

With our courage gathered, we purchased the necessary tickets to take us right up to the top of the Space Needle. I'd never been a big fan of heights, but there was no way I was going to let that tinge of fear get the best of me – who knew when I'd get the chance again?

"Honey, are you sure you want to go up there?" Mom wrenched her head to look up at the top.

"Quick, let's get in line before I change my mind."

We packed into the elevator with several other tourists. The ride to the top was so fast, it was hard to take it all in. We reached the top and exited the elevator to the open deck. For a moment, things seemed to be spinning in front of me. Slowly, I made my way over to the edge, and looked down across the metal railings that lined the observation deck. The view was phenomenal; the view was unobstructed for miles and miles. The rush of the city below us seemed insignificant – the normal hustle and bustle barely audible from that height. The limitless horizon made it seem like anything was possible.

While pursuing music remained a major focus for me, I was still working hard to fulfil the necessary credits to get my high school diploma. The last year's journey to the light at the end of the tunnel had been a bumpy one. While English and social studies had proved easy for me, I still found math and science courses a challenge. So when I filed into the massive high school gym where I joined dozens of other students writing their final exams, I did so with some trepidation.

Rows and rows of desks were filled with students; the proverbial black cloud of doom that hung over the room was almost palpable. I sat down at a desk and pulled out my pencils and my good luck charm – a monkey keychain Grace had given me.

No pressure. I repeated the mantra in my head, but the fact was that my entire academic career came down to this one last exam. I calmed myself down with a deep breath in an effort to stop my hands from shaking.

As I poured over the contents of the test booklet, the questions seemed relatively easy—which meant one of two things. Either I had done a great job of studying, or I really had no idea what I was doing, and was destined for failure. A deathly silence fell upon the room, replaced only by the scratching of pencils as we collectively focused our minds on the task at hand.

As I finally closed the book, I felt my muscles relax and a tiredness wash over me, as I moved towards the gym exit. There was nothing else I could do now. What was done was done. There was nothing left now, but the waiting.

A few weeks later, a phone call came in that left Mom's visage painted with a veil of concern. She walked over to the table where I sat, the seriousness of the call's contents immediately clear.

"That was Cliff. Sandi is having seizures, and she's in the hospital. They're running some tests," she said. "She's sedated, but they're allowing visitors now."

The news landed on me with a thud. Sandi had seemed so healthy, so vital. She's been working tirelessly in her nursing duties on the AIDS ward of the hospital I'd frequented so often. It didn't seem possible she could be ill. And more than that, it didn't seem fair.

After Dad finished work the following night, we all piled into the car and headed down to the hospital to visit Sandi. When we walked into her hospital room, she was sleeping peacefully. She was hooked up to various machines and a camera designed to closely monitor her vital signs. Despite all the time I'd spent in hospitals, this was different. My eyes filled with tears, and a sick feeling settled in my stomach.

Sandi's mom sat next to her, brushing her hands gently. Even as she lay there, she was so beautiful. *It'll be okay,* I told myself as I tried to push all the *what-ifs* and worst-case scenarios out of my head.

After a few days, she was released and became a member of the dubiously *elite* club of the unhealthy. Her condition remained a mystery to the doctors, though. And while we all tried to enjoy our time together upon her release, it was difficult to dispel the worry and fear we all felt. As Cliff helped to steady her on the walk up to the house, she turned to me.

"Alison, I know how you feel."

It broke my heart to hear her say that. I wouldn't have wished those feelings on anyone; I would have done anything to take that pain away from her.

The holidays crept up on us quickly, and while Sandi was struggling with her new health concerns, I found my own health interrupting my attempts to enjoy the season. On Christmas Eve, I began to experience severe cramps, burning, and diarrhea – far more severe than anything I had experienced even when being weaned off the steroids. As Christmas Day came and went, Boxing Day arrived with no improvement to how I was feeling. So after seeing my GP, he soon referred me to a gastroenterologist, in an effort to finally get to the bottom of my stomach woes.

The day of the specialist appointment we entered the towering office building across the street from one of the few hospitals I hadn't been to. Dr. Explorer strolled in dressed in the latest fashions and sporting a pair of small, brown glasses that were the trend of the moment.

"I would like to run a battery of tests on you— including a colonoscopy and gastro-endoscopy. They involve inserting a tube fitted with a camera up into your colon and down your throat. You'll be sedated for both of them, so it shouldn't be uncomfortable. No worries."

No worries? It's not your orifices that tubes are exploring.

I'd had to fast for the gastro-endoscopy, and as I sat alone in the sterile green procedure room in the flimsy hospital gown, my stomach growled loudly—mostly out of hunger, but I'm sure partly from nerves. But as anxious as I was about the tests, I was eager to find an answer as to what was causing the cramps.

"Let's find out what's going on here," Dr. Explorer said. "Alison, please lie on your side."

"Bite down on this," the assistant instructed me. "It'll give our camera access and keep your tongue out of the way."

"We're going to give you the medication now," Dr Explorer said as she injected the clear fluid into my arm.

As the drugs took effect I started to feel like the doctor was speaking a foreign language – but yet I could still understand her. My answers to all her questions felt like they were coming out in slow motion; the rest of the procedure was a blur.

The next day was the colonoscopy. The prep for it involved fasting again, but it also required drinking a milk jug-sized pitcher of a clear, salty liquid—the result of which was that I staked out the bathroom as my temporary home for the next twelve hours.

"Kinda boring in there, huh? Let me fix that." Mom left the room and returned with a television tray, a chair, and a deck of cards.

"How about a Frustration marathon?"

I started to shuffle the deck only to have them fly out of my hands and spray out across the room. Mom and I devolved into a fit of laughter.

"What's all that giggling in there?" Dad asked from the other side of the door, which only made us laugh harder.

Needless to say, the experience of the colonoscopy did not rank amongst my top favorite moments, but once complete I at least felt a sense of relief that they might point me in a direction that would allow me to get past all of this.

When the results finally came in, I met with them with mixed emotions. While I imagined they could have been worse, they still weren't what I had hoped for.

"All the results point to is irritable bowel syndrome," Dr. Explorer explained. "There's no cure, and no one really knows what precisely causes it. I can give you some medications that might help ease the cramps and a laxative might also help."

While I should have been relieved it wasn't something more serious, I was crushed to find it was something permanent – something that would be with me forever. I'd so hoped that whatever had been causing my stomach woes would be something that could be fixed with a surgery or a medication. Not something that would remain with me all my life; not something that would steal away one of the few simple – and normal – pleasures I enjoyed with friends and family.

The news hit me hard; I felt like I'd been kicked in the stomach, both figuratively and literally. Piece by piece, I felt like my identity and my independence was being stripped away. Whenever I'd received bad news about my health, it had always taken me some time to adapt – to find a way to still be me while working past all the changes. But one of the things that often helped me to cope was the communal activity of eating. No matter how restricted my physical activity became, we could still all break bread together. But now that was gone.

While the medication did help calm the painful cramps, I found that many foods now caused me discomfort; spices, salt, anything freshly baked, fresh fruit and vegetables would all cause my stomach to rebel. Cooked fruit and certain vegetables were tolerable, but only in small amounts. Every day became an act of knocking off the list of foods my gut would tolerate, the consequences for transgression being hours in the bathroom dealing with burning nausea and pain.

The next two months found me sinking into a depression. The usual things that brought me joy, like my crafts and music, held no interest for me. My energy levels plummeted and I felt like a robot just going through the motions each day. For a brief moment at the drugstore, I found myself excited. On one of the racks full of pamphlets at the pharmacy counter, I found a brochure on irritable bowel syndrome. After having lived my life with a disease that few people in the world seemed to have – let alone understand, I felt a weird sense of happiness that I had a *regular* condition that was detailed in a drugstore brochure. But as I read the leaflet, my excitement dissipated – there was no magic bullet solution to be found in its pages, *normal* disease, or not.

While it took me some time to adjust to my new reality, as time passed I eventually came to terms with the new diagnosis. More than that, I realized that given the enormity of the challenges I'd already faced in my life, this new one represented more of inconvenience in comparison.

I needed to get my life back on track, and with high school graduation fast approaching, it was the perfect thing to refocus me. Along with this milestone came the requisite grad photos. I had the bonus of being able to get them taken at a private studio, rather than at a school like everyone else. But while many of my educational milestones had been reached through an alternate route, we made sure that I was able to attend on official graduation ceremony. Because I'd been playing catch-up so often, we got in just under the wire; had I been any older, I would have been ineligible to attend. So I had worked hard to ensure that I would not miss out this rite of passage. I desperately wanted to have the memory of that achievement for my own.

On the day of my grad ceremony I was greeted with an intense headache and an aching that spread throughout my body.

"Son of a seadog. Are you going to be able to go?" Mom asked upon seeing my face wince from pain.

"I'm not missing out. I'll rest all day and then load up on meds."

As the medication began to take effect, the marching band in my head took an intermission and by the time I reached the dressing room at the convention centre, my body began to relax. Students were rushing around me frantically, clothing themselves in the ceremonial robes. My gown was bright green, and as I slid it on and donned my matching cap with yellow tassel, the excitement washed away any fatigue and tiredness remaining. The kids bustling by were strangers to me, though. They were people I'd never met, never attended a class with, and never had the chance to get to know.

"Line up to march out for the ceremony. Alison, the individual behind you has agreed to push you out," the grey-haired organiser said. Mom smiled at me, and left to join Dad in the audience. As we all lined up to march into the conference room, I thought about all the times I had visualised receiving my diploma. In my mind, I had always seen myself walking across that stage – not being wheeled.

"Once in the room, the protocol is to stay in this order. Then you will go up to get your diplomas. Remember to change your tassel over to the other side, and to shake with your right hand. Congratulations, everyone," the organiser said. As we approached the many rows of chairs, I parked myself, and looked out ahead of me.

I'm here. I did it.

Mom and Dad were a few rows behind me, and further behind them sat Grace and Ivy. Unfortunately Cliff and Sandi hadn't been able to make it – she was having a bad day health-wise, something I understood completely.

Butterflies bounced around my stomach as the adrenaline pumped through my body, erasing any residual discomfort. As my turn approached, the school rep turned to me.

"Alison, we can carry you up the four steps if you would like."

"Thanks, but I really want to walk across that stage and receive my diploma. Can you be at the other end of the stage waiting for me?"

"Sure, we can do that."

At this point, the medication was starting to wear off and the room nearly fell into a spin several times, but I was determined that this was one childhood vision I was going to make a reality.

"Alison Neuman."

Immediately the rep helped me onto my feet. I steadied myself, held onto the railing and pulled myself up the few steps. The adrenalin had taken over and my pain had been temporarily abated. I walked over to the principal, shook his hand, got my certificate and moved the tassel over on my hat.

"Alison, way to go!" Grace yelled from the audience.

I stepped off the stage to the echoes of applause, and back into my comfortable wheelchair. As I caught my breath, the rep wheeled me back to my seat.

"Alison," she whispered to me, "congratulations."

It was a moment that I was uncertain would ever happen – a moment to savour. It was a lesson in perseverance, one that was hard-learned, but completely worth it.

It seemed only logical that after closing the chapter on high school that I move on to the next major milestone that every teenager dreams about – driving a car. I'd had my learner's permit for ages, but I had yet to get behind the wheel. In fact, I hadn't really given much thought to it at all, so I was surprised when one day Cliff had approached me with an offer.

"Hey Alison. Let me take you out, and teach you how to drive."

Oh my goodness. Really? Cool.

"Sure, let's go." I felt like I was literally buzzing with excitement.

"I think we'll go out to Grandma N's farm for practice."

"That'd be great," I said.

As we headed out to the farm, Cliff turned to me.

"So would you like some Valium before we start?"

"No thanks," I giggled. "Would you?"

He scowled at me.

We listened to the radio. There was a truck in front of us, and the woman passenger was practically on the drivers lap.

"Oh get off him, and get a room, will you? He's trying to drive!" Cliff said as we watched a woman in the truck ahead of us practically mount the driver. We reached the gravel lane that led to my grandmother's house, and my brother slowly brought his truck to a stop and turned off the ignition.

"Okay, you drive now." He left the keys in the ignition, and got out. I slid over to the driver's side and waited for further instruction. He climbed in the passenger's seat, and turned to me.

"How much do you know?"

Nothing at all.

"I've never even started a car."

"Place your foot on the brake, and turn the key."

"Now what?" I asked, placing my shaking hands on the steering wheel. There I sat with my dry mouth, heart racing, and the truck engine running.

"Shift the truck out of park and into drive – but keep your foot on the brake." With my foot on the brake I moved the cold metal gearshift.

"Now drive. You don't have to go fast."

As I pushed the gas, the truck jerked forward. We both slammed forward in our seats. As I looked ahead down the road, I began to panic at the sight of several houses and a sharp turn in the lane; I slammed on the brakes.

After having stopped a few moments, I slowly negotiated the turn down the gravel lane. The truck kicked up dust, and vibrated from the loose gravel underneath the tires.

"Alison, take a turn by the milk house, and go out by the silage pit."

Slowly, I turned the steering wheel, and navigated between the houses and blue-green spruce trees towards the milk house.

"Try not to hit the milk house."

As the bumper of the truck approached the red brick milk house, I quickly hit the brakes. Cliff pushed himself back into the seat.

"Cliff, tighten your seatbelt! Do you want to drive now?" I asked him.

"Nope. Put it in reverse, back up a bit, and try again," he said patiently.

I put the gear shift into reverse, gently put my foot on the gas, and looked over my left and right shoulders as I backed up. Then, with my foot placed firmly on the brake, I put the truck back in drive, and eased my way forward.

The road ahead could hardly be called a road at all – it was more of a grassy area with some tracks worn down in the the mud. Slowly, I advanced the truck into the ruts and drove past an old fence made of wire and poles flaked with paint.

I was bordered on one side by grassy green hills, and on the other by mucky sloughs.

"Avoid the sloughs, okay?" Cliff laughed.

"I'll try." I had a death grip on the steering wheel.

Then I drove out by the silage pit where my uncles were working.

"Turn here, and take that road Alison."

He pointed to the right.

"But look how sharp that turn is, I'll go into the slough!?"

"This is a farm. They have tractors for that," he answered plainly.

With his urging I drove down the road, the truck getting closer and closer to the fence. All of a sudden the truck hit a patch of mud and slid into the wire fence. I panicked – just beyond that fence was a massive slough.

"Cliff! Now what?"

"Just back up, and get back onto the road," Cliff said calmly.

I put the truck in reverse and pushed the gas pedal, but the truck stubbornly dug down, and would not budge. By then my arms and hands were sore.

I turned to Cliff.

"Could you drive now? I'm wiped."

I slid over to the safety and comfort of the passenger's seat. Cliff sat down in the driver's seat and backed up and out like it was nothing.

After hearing about my attempts with Cliff, my dad got on the bandwagon as well, and offered to take me out for some practice.

We opted to head out to Grandma N's again; it seemed the best place to incur the least amount of damage. Once again we drove on the bumpy front lane, only this time when Dad approached the fence, he got out of the car and opened it up. We drove up over the hills and into an open grassy field that stretched out as far as the eye could see. The sounds of crickets, birds, and the wind blew past us through the windows. Dad stopped the car, moved the seat forward.

"There you go." he said. "Now you drive." I climbed into the driver's seat, and I started up our car without any hesitation.

"Drive over there, and then turn."

The car bumped up and down on the uneven ground, as I turned and straightened it out.

"Now do the same over there."

I was etching a never-ending pattern of figure eights across the field, when suddenly I saw a blur of brown and beige out of the corner of my eye. Of course, I knew it was a farm, and there were various types of inhabitants throughout – but somehow it hadn't occurred to me they might appear during my driving practice!

"It's only a gopher. There are lots of gophers out here," Dad said.

"But I don't want to hit one!"

"You won't. Don't worry."

The afternoon of leisurely driving in the country had suddenly begun to feel like playing Super Mario Cart. In the video game when you hit a gopher, they stayed with you, making irritating noises as you raced along. I knew the reality of hitting a gopher would be a lot more bloody, and a lot less pleasant.

My arms started to ache from the tension of holding the steering wheel, and it was becoming harder for me to manage to keep control of the vehicle.

"Dad, can we stop now? I've had enough driving for today."

"All right, if you're sure you've had enough. Let's go drop in on Grandma N."

We parked the car, and walked up to the house, where my Aunt Richelle let us in.

"Mom is resting. But I'll go tell her you guys are here," Aunt Richelle said.

No sooner had she finished her sentence than Grandma N walked into the kitchen wearing a bright summer dress. A smile spread across her face when she saw us. Within minutes, the two of them had seated us at the table with cheese, sausage, bread, cherry gelatin, and farm cream.

"Alison was out scaring the gophers just now," Dad said.

Grandma N and Aunt Richelle started laughing.

I was glad to have gone out for a drive, but didn't want to drive in that field again.

Chapter Fifteen

As I became more serious about singing, I realized that I need to develop my skills and take lessons from a professional. Mrs. D's long hair was pinned up in a tight bun, not a hair out of place, and her dress was pristine –without a wrinkle in sight.

As she introduced herself to us, Mom wheeled me into the studio, and parked me on the throw rug that sat next to her piano. The room, well furnished with antique furniture, and the large windows provided, had a clear view of downtown and the river valley. As Mom left to get some coffee, I perused the various photos and posters that adorned the walls.

"That's me and the cast," she said, smiling and pointing to a poster from *Cats.*

Mrs. D wasted no time, and we dove right into a variety of musical warm-ups as she introduced me to her musical language of "ro ree rahs" and "lo low lee lays." Her voice was clear, strong, and she had absolute control over it.

At the end of the class, she approached me with an offer.

"There's a musical festival in the spring. If you are up to it, maybe you'd like to enter."

"Sounds interesting."

"I'll tell you upfront – it might be a bit of a challenge for you to get the kind of breath control you need, while sitting, but I think we can figure it out."

And so for the next several weeks I worked towards this new goal. We'd decided on "*Hopelessly Devoted to You*" and "*Part of Your World.*" Every week of practice worked to entice my lungs to take deeper breaths. And every week the notes and phrasing became less of a challenge. But what made Mrs. D's classes so valuable was not just her technical expertise, but her passion for performance.

"Find the meaning, the emotion in the song, and convince me. Perform it," she said.

So locked in my room each night, I worked towards finding that passion within me, and expressing that vulnerability through each note and each phrase.

While I felt my self gaining strength in my voice, the arthritis had sapped my strength elsewhere. It had embedded itself in my right wrist, and turned it down into a useless 'L' shape, and my hands – unable to twist out of the claw-like shape – got caught on everything.

Dr. Sunshine suggested we make an appointment with a surgeon to see if anything could be done to improve it.

Dr. Gadget strolled into the room, and gently reached his hand out to shake mine, and Mom's.

"Alison, may I have a look at your wrists?"

He squatted down, and gently flipped my hand and wrist over in an effort to assess my mobility and flexibility, before looking at my X-rays.

"Alison, I think we can do a surgery that will make some improvements in your wrist. It will involve placing a titanium rod in it with some screws to hold it straight in a fixed position. It will limit your rotation, and it won't flex up and down anymore; so you'll have to wear a cast."

"For how long?"

"Two or three months. But I have to tell you though, that sometimes the rod doesn't take, and infection is a possibility. Usually things go just fine, and we give antibiotics to try and prevent any problems; but I want you to think about it before you let me know your answer."

A decision this big required some thought. Especially given that this was really the first major health decision I was facing on my own, as an adult.

"Mom, would you have the surgery?"

"Honey, I think I would, but I'm not the one who has to go through all of that. But Dad and I will support you whatever your decision."

I tried to weigh out all the pros and cons of having the surgery. It was winter, and the way the fingers were bent I couldn't wear gloves or even mittens, in this cold – so many of the cons were obvious. That being said, I still used my right hand to write; but there was always the possibility that my hand might worsen, rendering writing improbable. In the end, surgery seemed the best option, despite its risks.

Dr. Gadget gave me added confidence in my decision.

"While I'm in there, I might even be able to help your fingers a bit and give you more mobility, by scraping the scarring off the tendons."

During the weeks before surgery, I practiced writing with my left hand in the hopes that I might be able to rely on it during my wrist's temporary immobilization. Not surprisingly, my writing looked like the scrawl of a child just learning to write – but it was workable.

On the eve of the operation, I tried to relax. I tried not to entertain any thoughts of complications, but that didn't stop me feeling somewhat maudlin during my time with family and friends. That evening, Grace called to wish me well.

"How are you doing?" Grace asked.

"Not nervous at all – thought I would be. How are you?"

"Good. I'll be thinking about you tomorrow. You're my best bud, like a sister. Don't leave me, okay?" Raw emotion emoted filled her voice as she sniffled.

"That goes both ways, buddy. Besides, you're not getting get rid of me that easy."

"I'm holding you to that," she laughed.

Chills traveled through my body. I hated getting up this early anyway, and the added nerves for the event had made me a bit of a wreck for the ride to the hospital. It felt like we were going in slow motion; the lights from oncoming vehicles acted as beacons in the darkness ahead. I felt numb, rather than scared.

Once in the hospital room, the clock and I played the waiting game. Outside the window, light white snowflakes were falling peacefully – the light dusting was just enough to slow the Monday morning rush. I felt as though the world had stalled, as the hours stretched out before me.

"Mom, I hope I'll be able to stay in the singing competition."

"We'll have to see about your recovery."

My performance was scheduled for a month from now.

I hope I'm doing the right thing having surgery. I could leave now and no one would know any different.

I took a deep breath and tried to let the negativity exit my body as I exhaled.

Mom and I sat waiting across from the operating theatre for what seemed like hours. I looked over at her, struck by how much her presence in that cold room meant to me. During everything we'd been through, the whole course of my life and illness, she'd been a superwoman.

At the threshold of my first major medical intervention as an adult, our relationship was passing into a new phase. I recognized her not only as my mother, but as my best friend. She'd been my stalwart companion, my confidante. On the days where I felt I could not go on, she was there with a smile – giving me a reason to get out of bed. She knew when I needed silence and just the touch of her hand for comfort. I was truly blessed.

"I wish the surgery was already underway."

"It will be soon." She rubbed my arm with her warm hand.

"Okay Alison, we can take you into the operating theatre now," a nurse announced.

Mom and I gave each other a quick hug, and said our '*I Love Yous*,' before I was driven into the room, and Mom disappeared down the hallway.

Once in the theatre, I was introduced to the people in the room.

"Alison, are you cold? Would you like a heated blanket?" asked an assistant whose curls poked out from under her operating scrubs

"Yes, please." The cool temperature of the room had started to seep in under the sheets. The blanket was soft and comforting.

Then Dr. Gadget came in.

"Alison, we're going to fix the wrist and try to fix your fingers today. Did I tell you if there was not enough bone that we would borrow some from your hip?"

"No."

Geez, I hope not.

"Well, we probably won't."

Dr. Gadget patted me on the shoulder.

It still would have been nice to know about that possible-hip-business before I'd been wheeled in.

Muffled voices and the beeping of machines bombarded my ears. As I pulled my leaden eyelids apart I looked out on the rows of stretchers and sleeping patients.

A smiling nurse was working on me.

I felt peaceful and exhausted.

"Alison, you are in the recovery room. There is an oxygen tube in your nose. Are you in a lot of pain?"

"Um no, not right now."

Fight the exhaustion. Look at your wrist. But the energy wasn't there.

I drifted in out of sleep briefly, awakening when she checked in on me.

"If it starts to hurt, you let me know."

I didn't think my arm was hurting, but in my dazed state it was hard to perceive much. My arm was resting on a pillow. The wrist, and most of my hand, was covered in a brown elastic bandage and a half cast.

With all the wrapping, it seemed to have ballooned to twice its regular size.

Soon I was awakened by pain. My fingers throbbed, and a pain in my wrist pulsed with each heart beat. It was unbearable. Tears ran down my face.

"Can I please have some medication? My wrist hurts."

"Sure dear, I'll go get you some."

I slept most of the day, but Mom never left my side. Dad joined us after work; and they stayed with me until visiting hours were over, and I went back to sleep.

I awoke at one point to find myself in such an uncomfortable position that I needed to move the head of my bed up. Maybe it was my highly medicated state, but my electronic bed suddenly became a source of great joy and entertainment – with each push of the button the bed whirred my head and feet up and down, never ceasing to amaze me.

Whee!

The following morning a young and enthusiastic nurse came in.

"Alison, you have to go have X-rays taken of your wrist. I'm excited to work with you – your case sounds so interesting!"

As she spoke, her voice sounded like a cassette being played at half-speed. Her warped words echoed around in my head. *Why is my head doing that?*

Dr. Gadget came in.

"Alison, how are you today?"

"Good, I think."

"You did great. We didn't have to take any bone from your hips. The metal rod and screws went great. I tried to fix some of the scarring in your fingers

163

while I was in there, and in time we'll see how successful we were. Would you like to go home today?"

"I don't know. What do you think?"

"Well, since the surgery was successful. Resting at home in your own bed might be more comfortable. I could arrange that."

"S-sure, whatever you think is best."

"I'll sign you out and leave a prescription for some painkillers at the nurse's desk. Be sure to wear the sling when you're up."

I returned home to the comfort of my quiet room and sunk into my own bed. The only sounds I heard were Mom and Uncle Ingmar quietly talking. Unfortunately, the medication they'd prescribed for the pain wasn't working; and like clockwork, one hour after taking the pill, my wrist and hand started to burn and throb.

The medication might as well have been a water pill; something is wrong.

I looked down at my hand to find it swollen and red. *Is it supposed to look like that? Why am I so hot?*

I tried to keep my concern to myself. I thought that if I could just hang on a bit and not let the pain get to me, eventually it would ease off. But by lunchtime the next day, it clearly wasn't going away by itself. I asked mom to call Dr. Gadget, who suggested we come into the hospital clinic for a look.

The drive to the hospital seemed especially long today – like we missed every traffic light, and no car was in a hurry. As each long minute on the road passed, the pain grew worse, and the throbbing became more intense.

When we got to the clinic, I was immediately sent off for X-rays and sat waiting in an examination room, the painkillers having long since worn off.

Dr. Gadget entered the room.

"I hear your wrist is very painful. I'd like to get my assistant to unwrap your arm and I'll come back and have a look at it."

His assistant came into the room, wearing a designer T- shirt and jeans, and started to gently unwrap the stretchy fabric.

I don't know what exactly I was expecting to see beneath the bandages and cast, but it certainly was not what I saw. My hand and fingers were swollen and the skin was a dark and scary red. It was tinged yellow from antiseptic, and an ugly row of stitches crawled down my wrist. It had never even occurred to me that I'd have a scar.

Dr. Gadget very gently held my arm and examined me. He looked up at me, cautiously.

"I would like to admit you into the hospital," he said, "to administer some antibiotics and give you some medication for the pain. It looks as if an infection has started; that's probably why the pain is so severe. What do you think?"

"If you can alleviate this pain, then let's do that."

We went down to admitting, and waited two hours for a bed to open up. Once I was settled in, a nurse came in and gave me a shot of painkiller. The moment it kicked in, I felt almost euphoric – not from a high, but because such a wave of relief swept over me. The pain level dropped from a ten to a six.

Mom stayed with me that afternoon, and when Dad got off work, he brought some of my essentials up to the hospital.

I glanced at the clock

I'm going to miss "Friends," and ironically, "ER."

The hospital room had a small television, but in order to get a signal you had to have a cable rep bring a cable box by. I'd been admitted so late, I figured that they'd completed their rounds.

A woman in a tan-colored uniform, emblazoned with the cable company's logo, walked down the hallway and glanced into my room. Her eyes quickly found the box where the television subscriptions were housed, and she immediately came into the room.

"I knew you must be the patient I was sent for, because when you saw me, your face lit up."

It's amazing how important those simple pleasures can become when you're away from home.

That first night, several hospital staff members unsuccessfully tried to get an intravenous started. After the young resident's last attempt, she said, "If we can't get one started, we might have to start a central line, because it's important to get the medication in your system."

I know I'm going to be sorry for asking, but I can't help myself.

"What is a central line?"

"A central line is like an intravenous, but we put it in your neck. Have a good sleep," she added on her way out

Like that's going to happen now.

Needless to say, it was a long night. The next day, Dr, Gadget came in, and we discussed why my intravenous medication hadn't been started yet. He decided to give it a try himself. After poking around my arm for a bit, he finally found a usable vein on my good wrist, and the medication began to work its magic.

As the infection lost its strength, the pain lessened; my doctors' appointments became fewer and farther between. With that gradual, but ongoing, improvement the time came to remove my cast for a new one. The saw they use always looks like it belongs on the set of a horror movie, and it cut the cast like it was paper.

Underneath, my wrist was pale white with peeling dead and yellowed skin around where the incision had been; but the bone was beautifully straight. But while my wrist now looked like everyone else's, the bones were fused, and I had virtually no movement in the joint.

To improve the mobility, I was scheduled for physiotherapy twice a week. I had to dose up on painkillers before each session in order to keep the fingers from being too rigid or sore to work with. My therapist, Veronica would sit next to me and flex my fingers open and closed, bent and straight until, by the end of each session, my fingers ached and burned.

Even in hospital, I had tried my best to keep up with my vocal exercises. But as the date for the festival classes approached, I found that the constant need for medication, and my overall level of discomfort, had lowered my self-confidence quite a bit. Adding to that, this would be the first time I was going to be seated in my wheelchair. The fact was, the wheelchair was part of who I was – and I was tired of fighting it. I knew that the wheelchair was the key to my own personal freedom and mobility, and had nothing to do with the person inside.

When I got to the college where the competition classes were being held, I ended up spending the morning in washroom, and missing one of my performances. To try and salvage the remaining classes, I took a medication for my bowel and avoided eating altogether.

I made it to the later class, and entered the room where a grand piano sat, centre stage. The adjudicator sat some distance from the piano at a table in front of rows and rows of occupied chairs. As my name was called, Mom pushed me up to the front of the room. My accompanist was seated at the piano, and waited for my cue.

"My name is Alison Neuman, and I will be singing '*Part of Your World*.'"

I nodded at the pianist. I glanced at my feet, then up, and began to sing. My voice came out strong and clear. Yes, I was sitting in a wheelchair and had a casted arm, but from that moment until the end of the song, I was first and foremost a performer. As I finished the song, smiling faces reflected back at me from the audience. I thanked the pianist and returned to where we were sitting. Everything about my performance felt right; I felt *on*.

After all the scores had been tabulated, the adjudicator stood up in front of the room and assessed and critiqued the performance. The stern adjudicator closed her comments with:

"Alison, I award you first prize in this class."

No way.

My heart pounded with pride and excitement as she handed me my first place certificate. The adjudicator said more after that, but I barely heard a word.

"Congratulations!" Mom exclaimed with a huge hug.

"I did it, Mom. I finally did it."

"Honey, I knew you would."

Shortly afterwards it was time to get my final cast removed. Dr. Gadget started up the saw and made one careful cut at a time. The fresh cool air welcomed my wrist back to the world. My wrist was slim to begin with, but it was slimmer now, and covered in peeling skin.

As I examined the wrist I couldn't even remember how crooked my wrist was before. The hassles of having it catch on everything, and getting wrenched painfully, were just faint memories.

I continued physiotherapy for several weeks.

"Your fingers have reached the point," Veronica eventually said, "that we're not going to see any further improvement; so you don't need to keep coming."

Part of me was thinking 'yes!' But I was also disappointed that so little progress had really been made. The straightening of my wrist had given me more strength, but the surgery hadn't given my fingers any more mobility.

The surgery and recovery behind me, I was trying to figure out where to go next with my music career. I was now twenty-three years old; and I still wanted to work towards being a singer. It was almost kismet then, when a brochure came to our house advertising musical theatre classes at The Citadel Theatre.

Maybe that's my next step.

I couldn't recall ever seeing a musical starring an actor in a wheelchair, but I didn't let it deter me. Granted, the acting component would be relatively new to me, and would no doubt be a challenge. *Quick, enrol now before you lose your courage.* And I did.

Before classes started, we were all called individually by the course's piano accompanist, and asked to prepare a song to sing for the first class. Despite the fact that I'd sung in front of strangers numerous times, there was something more daunting about the prospect of being expected to inject the acting elements into the performance.

Oh well, I don't know anyone here, so I can always just leave and never return.

The leaves had begun their transformation from green to orange and yellow, and the air had a chill the week my classes were set to begin. I had been practicing *"Part of Your World"* for a week, but I still found my stomach churning upon my arrival at *The Citadel*.

My fellow students took the stairs to the classroom, but I was shown the special stage elevator. I felt a rush of excitement at this *backstage* look at the theatre area. There were green rooms replete with coffee pots, refrigerators, a comfy-looking couch, and racks of costumes. Once outside the elevator, we drove past various props lining the narrow hallways.

Full mirrors covered the walls of the large classroom. Mats were set out on the floors, and several folding chairs were set up next to an upright piano.

"Let's get into a circle and then we'll get ourselves warmed up." Our teacher, Teagan, had a naturally dramatic personality, and did everything with flair.

He stretched his arms up above his head and proceeded to show us a variety of exercises designed to loosen us up.

"Alison, just do them the best you can."

"Next, let's warm up those vocal cords. I want you to sing the phrase, '*rubber baby buggy bumpers.*' Try to keep up with the piano on speed and scale." It seemed easy enough, until the scale quickened in pace. Before we knew it, the mess of words had become a complete tongue twister, and the class broke down in laughter. The silliness helped ease the tension; it was hard for anyone to remain shy or guarded after that. We then went around the room and each student briefly stated his or her reason for taking the class.

"Now we can get into the performances."

Teagan pushed the chairs to the back wall.

"Any volunteers to go first?"

"I'll go second!" I volunteered.

But after the first student's clean and moving performance, I was second-guessing my decision. *I can't follow that!*

After the applause, the teacher turned to me.

"Alison, come on up."

I pulled myself over to the piano, and gave the pianist my sheet music.

"Are you ready?" Kari, the pianist, asked.

"I think so." I pulled myself towards the middle of the room. The piano player started, and as the intro played, I studied the tiles on the floor to calm myself down. I looked up. My voice rang out strong, and I lost myself in the moment and the music. When I was done, the students applauded, and I picked up my music.

"That was great. Very moving," Kari said.

"Thanks."

At the end of the class another student came up to me. "Your performance gave me goose bumps and chills!"

It was the boost that I needed; I wouldn't be running out never to return. And as it turned out, I was a bit of a trailblazer: Keri informed me that I was the first person in a wheelchair to take the class.

On one of the days where we'd had an afternoon workshop, mom and I came home to a ringing phone. As I put my coat away in the hallway closet, I knew by the tone of Mom's voice, it wasn't good news. Mom hung up the telephone and sat down in silence.

As the October chill of winter crept in and everything surrendered to the cold, so too had my grandmother.

"Was that about Grandma N? Did she …?"

Tears began to stream down my face before the news was even made official. Her frail body had been weakened by the stroke, but it did not diminish the impact of the news.

"Yes," Mom said.

As we made our way out to the farm after Grandma N's passing, it was clear that the farm had already come to represent something very different to me. The feelings I'd once had on the approach to the farm had changed, now that she would no longer be there to greet us with a cup of tea and a bounty of baked goods.

Once on the main road to the farm, the car shook as it kicked up gravel and dust behind us. The house was hidden behind rows of spruce trees, and the swing on the porch was crowned with colorful flower boxes. On a clear night, the stars would twinkle, and you could look out for miles. The only sounds to be heard during the day were birds chirping, crickets clicking, frogs croaking, and geese honking.

As we parked at the side of the house, Grandma N's dogs ran up to greet us. Between wiener roasts in the fire pit and the family gatherings at Grandma N's house, going to the farm had always felt like going home. Now as we drove out there, the same big red barn shadowed her house, but the wood seemed much more faded. And now instead of feeling a sense of peacefulness, I just felt emptiness.

The farm that had once been my second home now felt empty and strange.

Even though she had lived a long life, her death had reminded me how short and fragile our existence on this planet was.

Back at the musical theatre course, we were working towards a final spring production of "*Brigadoon.*"

"I'll be giving everyone a solo and some chorus work," Teagan informed us.

I was paired up for a duet with a talented young woman for "*Waitin' For My Dearie.*" But with my own background, I was finding it challenging to understand my character's motivations. The character didn't want to marry someone because she was getting older, whereas I wanted so much to meet and begin dating. I wanted to be loved by someone other than my family, and I simply couldn't relate to her.

"Alison, try to convince us your character is not crazy for not wanting to marry just anyone," Teagan said.

Try as I might, acting still wasn't in my comfort zone.

Pushing my limits even more, my solo was in a higher key than I was used to. A week before the show, I was practicing when my voice broke on a note, and my throat began to burn. Every subsequent warm-up revealed that I couldn't travel up the scales any more. My voice either wouldn't come out at all, or it would hit the threshold and squeak. I had to rest my voice as much as possible, which did not allay any of my anxieties in the run-up to the show.

As Showtime grew closer, Teagan approached me after rehearsal one day.

"Alison," he said. "The stage has stairs."

My heart sank at what words he might utter next.

"But I've talked to the props department, and they are going to build a ramp. We've dubbed it the Alison Neuman ramp," Teagan said.

I was thrilled; inclusion wasn't going to be an issue.

That evening, I broached attendance at the production with my Dad. While he'd always been supportive of my endeavours, the theatre wasn't exactly his *scene.*

"Dad, could you come to our class production? It's in the evening after work."

He grinned.

"Sure. I'll get educated in the theatre."

And so the last person you'd expect to see in a theatre was sitting there with my Mom, cheering me on. The show went off brilliantly, and while my voice had not fully recovered, I'd managed to work around the problems.

I'd been mortified at the thought that I might let anyone else in the cast down after we'd worked so hard, but as we took our final bows, I knew that we'd all put on exactly the show we'd hoped to. It was a bittersweet moment, thrilled as I was to have been able to participate in the kind of production I never thought my condition would allow me to – but it was a moment tinged with sadness at the fact that it had all been temporary; it was unlikely I would ever get to work with any of these people again.

As fun as the experience had been, musical theatre generally requires a level of physicality that I simply didn't possess and could not acquire. So I decided to focus myself more heavily on my music. I started to take classes which were being offered by a well-known artist-manager, to try and build my knowledge of music and the industry.

The weekly classes taught us about image, marketing, the independent route, and agencies. On one occasion we were visited by Doug, an independent artist who worked in recording. In his leather jacket and jeans, he certainly looked the industry *part*.

"You can totally make your own disk, and release it. With a computer and your instruments, you can record, burn, and sell CDs," he told us. "The quality can range anywhere from the lower end to the higher, depending on that all important question of cash flow."

No way. I don't need a record company? Now if I only had a computer and some cash.

175

Now, I had hope. Hope if I didn't fit into the kind of artist image a label wanted, I could still make it happen. I'd never seen a singer in a wheelchair but in general, I was finding that people were receptive to me. I doggedly pursued every audition open to me, and I finally nabbed a round of auditions for a paid gig at a summer festival. There's nothing quite like getting that first paycheck for doing something that you love; and I finally had a shot at getting there.

Backstage at the gig, nervousness and excitement swept over me like a rush of crisp mountain air. You could almost smell the heat coming off the spotlight; and as I traveled to the center of the stage, I stirred up dust that floated up towards the lights like stardust. My name was announced, and a thunderous silence spread across the audience. My heart was beating up into my throat, and for a moment my mouth became completely parched.

I'd taken some medication to allow me to stand and walk a few steps. The stage boards creaked under my feet, and the spotlight held my dream in its warm grasp. Unlike other auditions that were held behind closed doors, this one was a performance in and of itself, with judges and a full audience eagerly watching.

I nodded for the background track to start and looked out at the faceless audience. A momentary panic hit me when it felt like my lips were moving but no sound was coming out. But what started out as just a breath came out as a sweet note. While I was on stage, I was one small voice, I was free, I was whole; where expressions of pleasure, joy, or surprise lit up the audience's faces, I was home.

As it goes in the hard-knocks world of the music industry, I was not chosen for the job, but their support and encouragement was worth the experience. Every audition and every rejection builds you up for the next experience and gets you that much closer to a 'yes'.

Chapter Sixteen

At one point, I started to realize that while I'd been spending so much time on my creative life, I had been neglecting my social life to a certain extent. Your twenties are supposed to be the chance for you to *live it up* and be out there, socially. But finding activities to engage in, that weren't limited by my health, was easier said than done. And I often felt that rather than limiting social opportunities for my friends, it was easier just to stick around home.

One day Grace and I had gone out for a drive.

"Alison," she asked me, "what are you doing for Canada Day?"

"The same thing I do every year – nothing."

"I'll take you down to see the fireworks, and the bridge waterfall. You have to see it."

Anyone from Edmonton knows that the high level bridge on Canada Day is one heck of a spectacle to see. Thousands of people line the edges of the river valley as the once-yearly watershed off the bridge is lit up before a massive fireworks display.

It seemed bizarre that in the course of the decades I'd lived in Edmonton, I'd never once seen it. I imagine it was just one of those things I thought would be too difficult for me to manage. But Grace would have none of it, and on July 1st, we drove downtown.

"We'll try and get in the lane so we can go on the bridge. That's best for the total effect. Ugh. This traffic is nuts!" Grace said as she turned up the radio in an effort to distract us from the gridlocks.

We inched ever closer to the bridge, singing at the top of our lungs, before we made it up onto the bridge deck just in time to see the water fall into the river.

"Oh wow." I said, before looking quietly out our window.

Grace turned her attention to me.

"You okay, Alison?"

"Yup. I just thought I'd never get to see this."

A truck passed us with two men teetering perilously in lawn chairs in the cab. Like scores of other people they had large maple leafs painted on their faces – they were screaming and waving a large Canadian flag.

"Fireworks next?" Grace asked.

"Absolutely."

"I know a good spot – the area is open, and we can see the other side of the riverbank clearly."

We parked the car, and listened to the radio as we waited for the sun to sink beneath the hills. The area ahead of us started to fill up with spectators sitting on the grassy area on blankets and folding lawn chairs. Helicopters flew back and forth across the river valley as we waited.

"They should be going off soon. Let's get out of the car, and we can see better. We'll have a full view of the sky that way," Grace said, as she came around and opened the door for me.

The dark night sky was already filled with the twinkle of the first evening stars. The cool air tiptoed across my face, and Grace tuned the car radio into a local station that was broadcasting music to accompany the fireworks. Suddenly the sky exploded with bright red and white, showing starlight on the crowds of people lining the banks of the valley. The combination of colors and music was mesmerizing. The crack of the fireworks and the faint aroma of smoke left in their wake could never be captured by a photograph. I had a faint recollection of seeing a display when I was small, but nothing compared to what I saw that night.

As I tried to make more of an effort to connect with the friends who'd stood by me, throughout the years, I realized that I'd need to start thinking again about my education. I loved singing, and I'd continue to pursue it; but I knew that I had to make other plans as well. It was a hard road to hoe, and I knew far too many talented artists had to supplement their income by waiting tables. I was also realistic about what plans my health might have in store for me.

My condition had the potential to create scarring of tissues that could limit my lung capacity, and render the future for a singing career somewhat uncertain. My disease was my body's driver, and I was just along for the ride. So I started looking around at a program that might be a good fit for me. Grant MacEwan College had an artists' manager program that seemed like it might work well for me.

I met with a college counselor who gave me my first introduction to the world of post-secondary education. I passed the clock tower that announced the entrance to the campus, and felt the energy of the students rushing to their classes. It filled me with a vitality and excitement; but deep down at the same time, I felt like I was that little girl in Grade Two – so fearful that I wouldn't fit in, that I would fail. I made my way with my mother to the Student Services area. As the elevator announced our arrival with a beep, I turned to her. She informed me that in order to get into the arts management program, I had to undergo a rigorous interview process, and she scheduled me in for the spring.

"Mom, I don't know if I should be here."

"Why on earth not?" she asked.

"I'm not smart enough."

"Don't say that. You belong here just like everyone else."

But moms are supposed to say things like that, and it did little to quell the anxiety bubbling up inside me.

When the date for the interview finally arrived, we headed to the downtown campus and were immediately met with two massive, heavy double doors. Had Mom not been with me, I never would have been able to break through these heavy doors. Traveling back and forth to campus was already going to be an issue; and coupled with the cost of tuition, those giant doors seemed to almost represent all of the barriers I would come up against in this venture.

The sounds of music and laughter, coming from the dance studios and music rooms, ushered us along several open pedways that looked down onto the basement of the college. I entered the small room that housed the program directors, and no sooner had I stopped my wheelchair, than the interview began.

As they asked me about my goals I grew flustered, as butterflies began doing the backstroke against the acid in my stomach. It quickly became apparent to them that this program might not be the right one for me.

181

"You have a dream of singing, and that is your dream," one of the heads told me. "Don't just give up on that dream, and settle to manage some else's dream."

It was the last thing I'd expected to hear from them. Most of the time people in the creative arts are being told that they need to give up on their idealism and get a *real job*. But here was a group of people telling me that my ambitions had not been misplaced.

So as soon as I left the interview, arrangements were made for me to complete the audition and testing process, required for admission to the music program. A few days later I entered the room for the written music tests, where dozens of hopeful students had been bunched in together.

"First there is a written test, and then a listening test. Good luck," a man informed us.

As I looked down at the sheet of musical notations I felt the same kind of terror I experienced when faced with a mathematic equation – the two really were so similar. The blank spaces where we were to fill in the missing notes taunted me, reminding me that I'd failed to undertake such an important component of musical education early on.

The fact that I couldn't read music hadn't really, to this point, affected me greatly. But now, when it really counted, I felt like I'd had the rug pulled out from under me. For a moment, I wanted to cry. I felt like such a fake. I peeked around the room at the other students, and not one seemed to be flailing in the way I was.

"Time's up. Now our piano player is going to play a note. Write down what note he is playing, and in what key. After that, we will move on to more difficult exercises."

I'd been floundering at the most basic exercises, and they grew exponentially harder as time went on.

You're clueless. You've blown this. Just put anything down on that paper.

"Now proceed to the open area, and sign up for your instrument or vocal audition."

As I walked out of the test room, I clung to the faint possibility that there might still be hope for me in this next portion of the process. Singing was my forte; so maybe this was something I could pull off – or at the very least demonstrate some competence in.

The vocal audition was held in a small room at the back of which sat the program heads. They cued my music, and I began to sing.

What happened next will go down as one of the most memorable experiences in my singing career.

As faculty met my gaze, the expressions on their faces were priceless; each and every one of them was agog – mouths gaping open, and eyebrows raised.

I wondered if a person in a wheelchair had ever auditioned for the program before, as clearly they had not expected to hear what came out of the mouth of the individual who had rolled in before them. I walked out of the room almost forgetting what had happened during the music test a few hours prior.

"How did it go?" Mom said whispering to me after she'd entered to wheel me out of the room.

"I nailed it."

Next, each student was taken individually to a small cubicle closed off with the soundproof sliding doors. After bumping my way into the space, I was instructed to sing what was on the sheet music before me. My heart sank. It would be another testament to my inability to read music. I had always learned a song by ear, and there was no way to fake my way through this. But instead of giving up, I sang a version of what I thought it might be.

"A good try, but that's not it," was the reward for my efforts.

It was obvious to everyone involved that the music requirements for the program were way above my head. My failed efforts to enter the program left me with a heavy heart, but on the upside, I wondered if having to eat, sleep, and be graded on music might not take away some of the joy it gave me. There was still an opportunity for me to reapply once I'd improved my skill set.

Until then, at the urging of my counselor, I decided to apply to the General Studies Program. Doing so would give me the experience of attending college classes, while balancing my assignments with my health issues. It would also be a great way to explore other subject areas that I might never even have previously considered.

I watched the mailbox for weeks for the response to my application to arrive. When it finally appeared, the old adage of '*thicker is better*' was borne out as I opened it up, and my eyes immediately fell upon the words "Congratulations."

Yes!

I was going to go to college like normal people. But *normal* people would not have immediately felt weighted down by the logistics of this new adventure. We would be able to get me a computer, which would certainly help me greatly, but there were still a tremendous number of considerations that would factor into attending regular classes. Still, there was time to deal with all those issues. And for that moment I simply revelled in the achievement.

My first day at college saw me at an evening marketing class. My lungs had been aching all day, and I'd had to stop en route to the class to catch my breath. But I refused to allow my health to disrupt this most memorable of occasions for me. After Mom wheeled me into the large classroom, she headed off to a coffee shop, while I officially embarked on my post-secondary career.

Dozens of students were seated around the curved desks that covered the multi-level room. Everyone seemed to be seated next to someone they knew, and I felt like the loner kid who had no one to sit with. But soon another girl sat next to me, and we struck up a conversation before the professor joined us. We were given a class overview of the various assignments, essays, projects, presentations and exams that made up the course curriculum. There was no *easing* my way into it. Instead, the contents of the course outlines hit me like a ton of bricks. What I'd thought would be a challenge, had now transformed into an overwhelming task, of what seemed like herculean proportions.

My stress only grew when the lung ache I'd been experiencing developed into a full-blown cough overnight. One of the complications of my poor health was that colds, especially coughs, rarely disappeared on their own. And what might be just an inconvenience for other people could quickly become dangerous for me.

So that Monday, I was forced back to the clinic, where Dr. Attentive gave me the bad news.

"Alison, according to the X-rays, the cold has spread into your lungs. We'll start you on some antibiotics. Hopefully in a few days you should feel a bit better, but if it changes or gets worse, you come back in."

A week later, in the middle of the night, I woke up hacking. All of a sudden my chest felt like it was being weighed down by an invisible elephant. I was wheezing and gasping, but I could neither expel nor inhale any air.

The house was silent; I could hear only the ticking of the clock and the distant sounds of the television in the living room.

Don't panic. Breathe. Go to Mom. If you pass out she'll call 911.

I walked unsteadily to her room, and stood in her doorway, unable to eke out enough air even to speak her name. Luckily, she heard me gasping and woke up. The distraught look of fear on her face, terrified me.

She led me into the bathroom, and leaned me over the sink. With her hand on my back, I focused myself on trying to cough. Eventually I was able to expel some mucus that made it slightly easier for me to breathe, but it was a frightening enough episode to send us back to the doctor. I was prescribed an inhaler; but the wheezing episodes continued, becoming so painful and difficult that every time I ate or drank, I almost immediately threw up. As the days progressed, I was getting worse, and there seemed to be no answers from the doctors. It became so bad, that one night at 3:00 a.m., we wound up at the emergency room.

After the usual number of unsuccessful attempts to get an IV started, they finally found a vein, and began to replenish all the fluids I'd lost and administer some anti-nausea medication. As I lay there the dancing elephant returned, and I began wheezing again. A panic attack struck me as my lungs tried furtively to get some oxygen into them. My heart raced. My chest and lungs gave into the sensation that an elephant was dancing on me. Wheezing leaked out.

Breathe.

Clear.

Come on.

"Honey, do you want me to go get help?" Mom asked.

I nodded my head, and Mom rushed out of the room. I had never experienced anything like it. I wanted to cough. I longed to cough, and move whatever was blocking my airway out of the way, but I just didn't have enough air to do it. There is nothing so frustrating and scary as being surrounded by air, but not being able to utilize a single particle of it. I felt like every time I was about to inhale, a vacuum was there stopping it from entering my lungs.

An assemblage of medical staff rushed in, and wheeled me out of the room, into another room at the end of the hall. I glimpsed the worried look on Mom's face as she followed us.

Mom, I love you. Everything will be okay.

The nurses and doctors were talking in anxious rushed voices. I was gasping.

A mask was placed on my face that emitted steam. Darkness began to close in on my eyes, and my body shook heavily with chills.

Will this be my last gasp – last breath?

I reached for the tissue box at the end of the stretcher, but couldn't reach it.

"What is she reaching for?" an elderly doctor asked as he rushed in.

"A tissue."

The slim nurse passed me one, and I wiped my nose. Suddenly the pressure began to ease, and gradually the simple process of inhaling and exhaling required less effort. After what seemed like hours, I could finally breathe easier.

"Don't do that again, okay?" the doctor said, "You scared me."

Mom echoed him.

"Yes, don't do that again."

"I scared myself. Could it happen again?" I asked.

"I don't think it should," the doctor replied.

After all that, I was finally given an appointment with a pulmonary specialist. But while I was out of the woods, so to speak, I couldn't even contemplate attending classes. I could barely get enough air, let alone the sleep necessary, to be remotely successful in my classes. So before the academic penalty date, I withdrew from my courses and was able to get a refund. I was not giving up on the idea of going to college, but I'd have to defer it, until I could get my health back under control.

The specialist, the small and gentle Dr. Gracious, put me on a new set of medications. An inhaler designed to help my lungs, and a nasal spray to help with the post nasal drip. He ordered an additional set of tests to see what, if anything, might be going on, but assured me in the meantime that I should see improvements in a couple of weeks.

We'd constructed an elaborate bed for me from an office chair and cushions, as I felt more comfortable in an upright position. I'd grown paranoid after the

188

episodes though, and at night I set the alarm to go off at precisely the hour when the medication was due to wear off. I was awakened every four hours to administer the meds, and Mom slept on the bed next to me to give me some added comfort.

As each week passed, my apprehension dissipated as episodes became more infrequent and less uncomfortable. I was far from a hundred percent, but I began to feel like I was back in control, to some extent.

A while later I was sitting watching reruns of one of my favorite shows, *"MacGyver,"* when I started coughing heavily. Before I knew it I had thrown up all over my socks, shoes, and the floor.

So gross.

Even with full box of tissues I wouldn't be able to clean up all the mess.

"Mom, can you help me, please?" I called out.

But before should she could respond the phone rang. The phone had been ringing a lot more lately, as along with my health issues, Dad and Uncle Ingmar had also been unwell. Relatives had been calling frequently for updates on our health

After a few moments, Mom came in my room – her face ashen.

"That was Cliff. Sandi passed away a little while ago. I have to go make a phone call. I'll be back." And without another word, she walked slowly out of the room.

Even as tears began running down my face, denial set in. *It must be some other Sandi. It can't be Cliff's Sandi. Our Sandi. They don't even know what's wrong with her!*

Soon Mom retuned, and wiped up the mess from a few moments ago.

"You mean our Sandi? But she's supposed to get better."

Mom nodded, and gave me a hug. I heaved with sobs.

"Is Cliff…?" I tried to say.

"Dad is going to bring him here," Mom said.

When Cliff came in the house, he was slouched over, his face was pale and his eyes looked empty. The twinkle, the light that was normally reflected in his smile was gone.

"Cliff, I'm sorry." I gave him a hug.

"Me too, Alison. Me too." He hugged me back and then just stood there – lost.

I wish I could take his pain away. Make everything be right again.

But I was helpless. The doctors had been helpless. We'd been helpless. And now, we were left alone, without reason, without explanation. Few words were said that night, and when I awoke the next morning, for a few minutes I could have sworn that it had all just been a bad dream.

The funeral home was calm and peaceful. A cousin escorted us into the front room where we were able to express our sympathy to Sandi's family. It seemed like a regular living room with a coffee table, couches and chairs. It opened out onto a second room, decorated to match the first, but with one surreal addition: in it sat a long, black coffin.

And then it hit me; Sandi was really gone. She was lying there, lifeless, in that box at the back of the room. I felt like someone had punched me in the gut as hard as they could.

Mom, Dad and I went closer to Sandi's body. Her hair was curly and she looked like she was sleeping. *Just open your eyes and smile. Just wake up. Please. There's so much I wanted to tell you. Tell you how much I loved you. Tell you how proud I was to have you in our family.*

As we entered the main chapel, the aroma of the wooden pews reminded me of a time when the world had made more sense. When I was small, and the world was simple – when family stayed with you forever.

"Alison, Sandi's family wonders if you could read 4:13-5:1 from Corinthians at the funeral?" Cliff asked me.

"It would be an honor."

The passage was speaking to the freedom of the spirit as it left the body, and it lent me some semblance of comfort. There was a tragic circularity as I thought on the reading I'd done at the wedding, only a few short years ago.

Sandi's death affected me more than I had expected. My whole life I'd been surrounded by people who were sick and ailing – and my own health had been a constant worry. But never had I expected someone who'd seemed so healthy to be stolen away from us so suddenly. In the months that followed, I found myself pulling away and putting up walls to protect myself.

The loss left me wondering what the point was to allowing people into your heart when they were all ultimately destined to disappear. Despite all that a relationship might give you, it would always leave you weaker when they left so unceremoniously. Was the price of having another person in your life, worth the darkness and emptiness that filled the soul and heart when they were gone?

Chapter Seventeen

One of the most difficult lessons that grief teaches you, is that life goes on. Despite the tremendous loss we were all experiencing I still had to go through with the pulmonary tests that had been arranged for me.

When we arrived I was led into the lab where a technician instructed me on the procedures.

"Alison, I'm going to put this clip on your nose. First, take the deepest breath you can; and then I want you to blow it out as long and as hard as you can."

The machine measured my lung capacity, and then recorded the outcomes on a graph filled with peaks and valleys.

"This next test is similar to blowing up a balloon. Take a deep breath and try to blow as hard as you can," the technician said. I took the deepest breath possible and exhaled as hard as I could, but I could barely get the balloon to expand at all.

"Now we need to take some blood from an artery to measure your blood oxygen level." The technician grabbed a syringe and slid over to me on the stool with wheels.

After several attempts, she became quiet.

"Sorry, I can't seem to find it. I'm gonna get someone else to try, and if they can't find it, we won't poke you anymore."

Story of my life.

Fortunately, another technician was able to find the artery without even so much as a pinch.

193

"Now we'll do the last test, and then you can go."

I was led into another smaller room, and parked near the counter.

"This test is to measure how sensitive your lungs are. We'll put a mask on you; first it will emit steam, then an irritant, and as the test progresses, more irritant will be added to test your lungs' tolerance. Let me know as soon as you feel discomfort."

The mask was put on, and immediately my lungs tightened.

"You are having discomfort, aren't you?"

I nodded.

She pulled the mask off my face and gave me a spray of a different inhaler.

"We're going to have to stop the test; your lungs are too sensitive."

When it was all over, and I met with the doctor, I asked him a question, point blank.

"Will the lung problem ever go away?"

"Alison, your lungs are weak and it may never go away. The problem was probably growing for quite some time before it became bad enough to notice. You may get some improvement with treatment, though."

I felt like it was a death sentence for my music dreams. With each breath I needed to sing, I felt as though my lungs were trapping that air inside me – I just couldn't expel it. I could do the occasional warm-up, but the massive constriction I felt in my chest meant singing would have to be put on hold, perhaps permanently.

At the start of spring, I began to experience unrelenting pain in knees. The previous May I had some seeping calcifications, but they'd disappeared, and I figured that they'd been a sort of 'one-off' occurrence. I never once considered that my illness was launching a full-out attack.

But as the pain increased, I had to do something.

"Mom, something is wrong. I think it's come back."

It was hard to articulate the sensation in my knees, but my whole body felt fatigued, like I had the flu, and I felt jittery. Something just always felt *off*, like putting your shirt on backwards. It was still your shirt, but somehow it didn't fit, or feel quite right. The calcium lumps began to appear all over my body, migrating at times, staying put at others. Once again I couldn't make plans for the next hour, let alone the next months. I spent more time at home in isolation, the pain becoming the guiding factor in all my decisions.

I was forced to revisit the medications from years ago, but in a liquid compound as pills had started to stick in my throat, choking me each time I tried to swallow them. I had to ease into the powerful meds so I could cope with the myriad side effects. The anti-inflammatory upset my stomach and yet another drug was needed to help combat those side effects. They robbed my appetite, and the food was flavorless in my mouth. My diet had already been limited by my IBS, and now it became an utter chore.

Some days, going out into a world to which I had once belonged was doable, and some days I couldn't manage it. Going out brought with it so many painful obstacles, that sometimes, it just didn't seem worth the effort.

I did my best to disguise the pain, trying to hide away my feeling that my life had been set in a tailspin. But Mom saw threw my façade, as moms are apt to do.

"I'm so sorry you're hurting and frustrated. I wish I could take it away for you," she said.

"Thanks, but I wouldn't wish this on anyone."

Most of my time was spent in my room either lying down, or sitting and watching television. I was grateful for the distraction that the television provided, because as much as I loved to read, holding my head in the position to do so resulted in throbbing pain, black spots in my line of vision, and headaches.

The nightmares that had plagued me as a small child also returned. I woke many nights sweating, heart racing, and crying. One morning I felt as though someone had stabbed me, and I awoke with a start. Golden light was shining in from the hallway but the house was silent. I was alone in the comfort of my room, and I knew that I was safe. But my brain wouldn't communicate to my racing heart that I needed to relax. Soon I heard Mom and Dad beginning the day. Once Dad had left for work, Mom came to my room.

"Good morning, honey."

"'Morning, Mom. Could you help me transfer into my desk chair?"

My legs throbbed as she moved me, and my entire body burned and ached.

"Would you like me to brush your hair?"

"Please." She gently ran the brush through my short hair. Strange how when you're ill, your vanity ebbs. I had recently cut off the beautiful hair that had previously fallen well below my shoulders. But your priorities shift, and I no longer gave a second thought to it. The meds had also affected its growth, and my thick brown hair came out in clumps on the brush. My head ached, but as she was so gentle, it felt good to have my hair brushed.

"Mom, could I have a painkiller?"

"Sure. I'll go crush it and bring it in," I watched television under the artificial lights of the room. The sun's light had proven to be too harsh for my eyes, and the blinds had been down for weeks. I swallowed the sour combination of crushed pill and water, and chased it with a spoon dipped in jelly to wash away the aftertaste that lingered in my throat.

Suddenly the room started to spin, and my mind slowed to a crawl. First a dark spot appeared in my vision blocking out my periphery, then the television screen disappeared. The auras always associated with migraines appeared next; it was like a small series of lightning bolts flashing before me, with small black pixels appearing in each. For twenty minutes the flashes grew larger and larger until they took up over half my vision. It moved around violently, and soon blue and pink pieces were flashing through them as well.

I knew this feeling well.

"Mom, my eyes are acting up. I'm going to lie down. I guess we won't be going out. I'm sorry."

"Don't be sorry," she said, helping me get back into bed. Chills ran up and down my body. She covered me up, and then turned off the light.

"Honey, if you need anything just call," Mom said.

"Thanks."

I was in the dark, but the aura flickering in front of my eyes would not let me rest.

I can't do this anymore. I need help.

We headed down the ramp, and into the warm summer air; I was on my way to see yet another specialist. The neighborhood was silent, and the lack of a breeze had made it eerily calm. The sun was intensely bright, causing me to squint, and wish I had brought my sunglasses. Mom and Dad were bantering back and forth, but I had no energy to contribute. I watched the scenery pass by, but everything seemed dull to me. My stomach churned, and my palms were clammy and cold from sweat.

Mom, Dad, and I sat in the waiting room on the multi-colored chairs that dotted the open space. I squinted with my blurry vision, trying to focus on the area around me.

"Alison, you can come in now," the receptionist said. Mom wheeled me into the examining room.

"Can you put on a gown? He will want to examine you."

The receptionist closed the door.

"Oh, I hate gowns."

"Me too, honey." She helped me force my stiff and sore joints to move. It seemed as though my bones were protruding, and my body felt unfamiliar. Then the door opened and the specialist, Dr. Respect, stepped in. He introduced himself and shook my hand. He was tall and spoke with a calming voice.

"First, I would like to check on your mobility." He pressed down on my joints, and had me push back against him. He was very gentle and respectful of my body – such a welcome change from so many of my previous doctors.

It was clear to him that my mobility was deteriorating despite all my efforts. It was a vicious cycle. First it was dangerous to move, and then when I

198

should move, it hurt to do so, so I didn't move. Eventually my muscles got weaker and mobility was lost. Now I couldn't walk or stand up by myself at all.

"Alison, I would like to order some blood tests. In two weeks when the results are in, come in and we can discuss them. In the meantime, if anything gets worse, let me know. And if you feel your system will tolerate it, try to up your anti-inflammatories."

Once again, my disease demanded that I polish up my acting skills with those around me. I was crumbling inside, but lest my friends think I had a one-track mind, focused only on my disease, I tried to mask my feelings. The truth was that I was on a long, slow journey of progressive deterioration, and the road back to health was even longer. But rather than even starting to broach the subject with my friends, my standard reply to their queries remained:

"I'm good."

My really good friends knew the truth, and pressed for it. One day Grace called me.

"Do you feel up to having a visitor?"

"Sure." I answered her, reluctantly.

Why would anyone want to hang around, or do anything with me, when I'm in this state? I'm not dependable.

Mom helped me get my painful and useless body off the bed, and into my wheelchair. As we entered the living room, my eyes squinted and watered as they adjusted to the light. When we drove by the hallway mirror, a skinny girl with a pale face and black rings under her eyes stared back at me.

Who are you?

Soon the doorbell rang, and Grace came walking over to me.

"Kick me out when you're tired, but I'm not leaving until then!"

While she visited, the only I aches I noticed were the stitches in my side from laughing.

A couple of weeks later we went back to scc Dr. Respect. In the office, the carpet color seemed so very bright – everything seemed so very bright.

"Mom, I wish it hadn't taken us so long to find Dr. Respect. I really like him."

But despite how glad I was to have him on my team now, my stomach was churning wondering if he would be the bearer of good news, or bad.

I sat up on the examining table when he entered.

"Hi, Alison. How are you doing?"

"I'm hanging in there."

He spread out my chart to review the findings. "The test results are fairly normal. The good news is your body is not over-producing calcium. The calcium moving around right now must be from a previous spell. Your blood count is low though, so maybe we can start you on iron. But we need to get your mobility back."

"Is there anything we can do other than the iron?"

"Maybe in September, if there is an opening at the rehabilitation hospital, we can get you in. If anything changes, call me."

"That sounds like a plan." I answered.

Then it struck me – something, I really wanted, and needed, to know.

"Out of curiosity," I asked, "do you know if there's a name for my condition?"

He looked at me, puzzled.

"No one ever told you?" he asked. "It's called dermatomyositis." He wrote the name down on a small piece of paper and handed it to me.

On that tiny scrap of paper over twenty years of struggle was etched. It didn't change what I was going through, or its effects on my body. But it lent a shape and form to my opponent. And the fact that I could finally name the enemy left me feeling like I was better armed for the battle.

Despite the fact that the test results had indicated that there was no new calcium production taking my place, my disease – which I'd now nicknamed 'Dermy' – was gaining a hold of my body in other respects, and I felt like I was losing control quickly. My room had become a prison.

Each migraine episode resulted in weight loss and made me feel lower and more hopeless than before. After a headache, it took me two or three days to recover fully from the aching and nausea. And with every headache, despite knowing what a slippery slope I was treading on, I eliminated a food from my already-limited diet. My twisted mind had justified this practice by suggesting that I *must have eaten something* that had ushered in its onset.

While I'd avoided stepping onto a scale, I eventually bit the bullet.

A blurry reading of 87 pounds appeared on the scale beneath my feet.

I haven't been this weight since I was twelve. Dermy, please go away. *This isn't living.*

On a Tuesday afternoon during lunch, the telephone rang with news of an opening at the rehab hospital.

"Honey, they're wondering if you can come in Monday at 9:00 a.m," Mom informed me.

"Yes." I answered defiantly, but with more than a twinge of angst.

I was always hopeful when these opportunities for help materialized; yet, so often I'd been disappointed at the limitations of that help. But at the bare minimum I knew that it wouldn't make things worse; it would be worth the effort on that account alone. Getting better might only be a few weeks away.

Chapter Eighteen

To try and put a positive spin on entering the rehabilitation hospital, I tried to think of it as a vacation. Unfortunately, the one thing I needed a vacation from, Dermy, was going to be my co-passenger on the trip.

Everything was packed the night before – my clothes, a pack of cards, a journal to write in, my medication, and my small tape player. We even packed my favorite cookies to hide in my room in case eating hospital food proved to be too much of a challenge.

Find your strength. You're going to need it.

Mom helped me get my jacket on, as Dad took my bag out to the car.

"Honey, everyone is here for you. If you can't find the strength, take some from us. You can do this," Mom said to me as we got in the car.

The hospital had been newly renovated – transformed from a dark brick box, into a more rounded shape with cream-colored siding. But more than a new façade, belying its unchanged interior, the experience had changed for me this time; I was now an adult. This time the front door was mine to exit whenever I chose.

I settled into my new room quickly; its window looking out onto a residential street, with a view of the airplanes heading in and out of the local airport, filled out the background.

"I'm going to leave, and let you get all settled," Dad said, giving me a me a hug.

"Thanks for coming!"

An airplane effortlessly glided across the sky, and both Mom and I gazed out the window.

"Cliff will like that," I said.

"Honey, you might have to fight him for this room with this view!"

Once the paperwork was filled out, I was thrown right into physiotherapy. Soon, a casual and perky woman named Paula came into my room, introduced herself, and completed a joint assessment. I then left to reacquaint myself with the facility and try to make myself more comfortable in the surroundings I would be calling home for an indefinite period.

I joined the other patients in the lunchroom. It soon became obvious that fitting this part of the ritual into my life would be a challenge. I ended up leaving hungry; there was nothing being served from the kitchen that wouldn't set off a bad chain reaction in my stomach. I returned to my room, and ate some of the cookies I'd brought to keep my strength up.

Fortunately we found later on that some of the fair downstairs included French fries – oddly enough something that passed my IBS test. Mom and I went down for supper. The French fries fed my hunger – the company fed my soul.

Later on, Dad came to visit, and we sat outside the front door at a nearby picnic table. The air was warm and fresh, and we watched the various airplanes, cars, and visiting patients, all coming and going. Then it was time to go. Mom helped me get ready for bed.

"I love you. We are proud of you. Feel free to call me any time."

"Thanks, Mom. Have a good night."

She gave me a hug, and walked out of my room into the hallway. In the darkness, I reacquainted myself with the sounds of a hospital – the nurses talking in the hallway, patients' bells beeping, and the air system going on and off. I used my cassette player to block out the unfamiliar noises in favor of the familiar musical voices that surrounded me at home.

Each weekday, everyone, both inpatients and outpatients, completed a near identical schedule, beginning at the pool around 8:30 a.m. and ending at 3 p.m. My bronchi were still causing me problems thus eliminating my pool time, so I spent that time in my room getting ready for the long day ahead. The days became a haze of therapy sessions on arthritis, instruction on using special aids like reachers, relaxation methods, and nutrition.

The days passed by quickly. Cliff came once a week, and we played games or sat outside to enjoy the fresh air and airplanes. They flew right overhead so we could hear the engines humming as they passed.

"This is a nice place – especially the view," Cliff said. "What do I have to do to get a room here?"

I always found it ironic that a facility where people were working to regain their freedom had a constant view of the planes that offered the same opportunity to travelers. All of us there dreamed of flying away from our current lives into something new and exciting.

On the fourth day, I awoke with a start. I was disoriented, and my thoughts swam as I tried to figure out had happened to wake me so abruptly. Then it became clear – a migraine aura was dancing in my view. For a moment, my heart raced and tears welled up.

Things were supposed to get better.

I gagged down some of the crushed migraine medication, and stole back to my bed, trying to hide from the sun that was peeking through the curtains. My heart sank.

A few moments later, Mom entered my room.

"Good morning Alison. Did you have a good night?"

"I woke up with a migraine."

Tears rolled down my cheeks; all I wanted was to go back home and climb into the safety and darkness of my own bed and room. I tried to keep a positive attitude, but this morning, made me wonder if maybe I couldn't beat Dermy. I was so angry. Here I was as an adult, trying to be strong; yet feeling like a weak little child unsure of the world around her, and scared of things that were beyond her control.

"Honey, son of a seadog," Mom said sympathetically.

"Mom, I'm sorry I won't be great company."

Mom sat next me on the bed, and put her warm and safe arms around me, giving me the strength to get through another episode. I spent the day throwing up and trying to keep the meds down, in an effort control the vice-like pain gripping my head.

"Alison, would you like me to stay with you tonight?"

"I don't want you to have to do that," I said.

But what I really wanted to say was, *'Mom, I'm scared. I don't think I can do this. I have no strength left. I just want to surrender. I don't have the strength to make it through another day.'*

"I'll stay tonight and maybe by morning things will be better."

Dad gave both of us a hug before he left, and Mom had a talk with the nurse.

The nurse came in a few minutes later, wheeling in a stretcher, complete with bed linen, and parked it next to my bed.

"Thought that we would bring in a bed for your Mom. That way both of you can be comfortable."

Having Mom there gave me peace, and it was the first night I actually slept well in the hospital. I knew now that I could ride out these episodes – that there would ultimately be an endpoint to them, but that being fearful of them was okay.

Just like with my previous hospital stays, the best part of the week came on Fridays when Mom and Dad brought me home for the weekends. As we drove away from the hospital, my body felt as if some invisible restraints were being loosened. Entering the house each time always reminded me where I came from and where I belonged. The silence, relative to the constant bustle and buzz of the hospital, was always somewhat disquieting for the first while. But home was safe, warm, and quiet with signs of comfort all around me.

If I wanted a moment to be alone and cry in the seclusion of my room, to let out all the fear and doubts without being judged, I could do that. Or if I wanted to blast my music and sing along, that was all right too. The flimsy privacy of the hospital curtains offered little such solitude. Having my own space once again, was priceless.

On my first weekend home, Cliff came over in the afternoon for a clandestine mission. We'd decided to give my parents an anniversary party they'd never forget – one that would make up for the lack of a formal wedding event when they'd first been married. So we were pouring over hotel menus at the dining room table, in an effort to craft the perfect dinner experience.

"What do you think, Alison? Turkey or roast beef?"

"I like turkey, and it is a white meat."

"Turkey it is. That was easy. The meal is planned," Cliff said laughing.

Next we needed invitations to send out to our guest list, so Cliff and I visited one of those *one-stop* speciality party stores. He wheeled me over to the table, and we looked through large heavy white binders filled with pages and pages of anniversary invitations.

"Well, what do you think, Alison? Have you found any you like?"

"I like these," I pointed to one with a burgundy trim.

"What is the color for the fortieth?" Cliff asked the woman who was helping us search.

"Burgundy is the traditional color," she said.

"So those ones, Alison?"

I nodded. We arranged for their printing, satisfied that the wheels for the grand event were now in motion.

My weekends were highly anticipated, and sped by in a blur of shopping, TV-watching, visiting, party-planning, and quality time with the family. Of course, I still had to fit in time to complete my physio and occupational therapy exercises in an effort to maintain strength and eke out some additional mobility. Just as it had when I was a child, the weekend's end rolled around far too quickly, reminding me how temporary this normalcy was.

While those weekends recharged me to some extent, I still noticed that I had stopped doing many things that I enjoyed during my stay at rehab. I hadn't turned on the computer in months. I hadn't been listening to music. I hadn't been doing my craft activities. I wasn't *living* anymore. I was just getting by.

The fatigue, the vision problems, and the pain had begun to overwhelm me. I just gave up. I felt completely directionless.

One day I happened to be talking with a physio tech, Audrey, who was making me hand splints.

"I would like to attend college again," I blurted out.

"Then you should do that. Why aren't you?"

"I don't know if I can. The college is large, and the old electric wheelchair I have doesn't work anymore."

"Of course you can! We'll just get you a new wheelchair." She met my gaze, and looked at me seriously. "What would you like to take?"

"Maybe writing."

"Then do it, Alison."

That's when I realized that the wheelchair issue had been a bit of an excuse. Bottom line was that I was scared of what Dermy might have in store for me if I went back. I was scared of all the issues my health presented; and I was scared that I wouldn't be able to do it – some good old-fashioned doubt.

The next day I made a trip to the orthotics department where they were going to make me some supports to help me compensate for my imbalance. It was hoped they'd be able to restore my ability to stand

"Alison, I'm going to wrap a casting material around your bare feet into a slipper shape. After hardening, I will peel it off," Audrey said. "Then we pour plastic into the molds to make the insoles to wear in your shoes."

A few days later my insoles were ready, and for the first time in many months, I was able to stand. My legs were weak, but now both my feet could meet the ground despite the bend of my arthritic knee. I had the ability to stand and in time, my legs might get strong enough to allow me to once again take a few steps.

Finally, Mom came into my room and greeted me with the sweetest words.

"Good morning, honey. Today is the last day."

I gave her a hug.

"We did it."

"*You* did it."

"I couldn't have done it without everyone's support."

"Shall we start packing?" Mom asked

"Let's get ready to blow this place," I said excitedly.

On the way home, Mom and I stopped off to meet my occupational therapist at a healthcare store and try out some different models of electric wheelchairs. I'd forgotten how much freedom these chairs gave me. Whizzing back and forth around the store, the wind blowing against my face, I felt empowered once again. Maybe this really was the start of a new era for me.

After selecting a new chair model for me, the drive home felt as though someone had turned the lights on inside me. For months I had been seeing the world in muted colors, but now everything seemed vivid and bright. I was expanding my diet again, and the vitamins needed to balance my system were kicking in. Although my iron was still low, my quality of life was improving in leaps and bounds, and I had hope that the energy I needed to make my life better was in sight. The list of daily activities I could perform by myself was growing

As we drove past the North Saskatchewan River, my eyes filled up with tears.

I'm still here.

At that moment it felt as if I was starting my life over again.

It was proving to be a challenge to fit in my demanding exercise schedule from home. In the hospital, my day was planned down to the second, but at home I had the normal demands of life to contend with. But the fact was that those exercises were what allowed me to keep up with those demands; they were what kept me moving, period. Honestly, it took me time to adjust to having some semblance of freedom again.

In addition, Mom and Dad's anniversary celebration was fast approaching, and Cliff and I were anticipating being able to see them have the reception of their dreams. It may have taken forty years, but we were going to make it happen. The days that followed were a chaotic rush of errands in preparation for the big event.

Finally, Saturday – the big day – arrived. I awoke that morning with a knot in my stomach in the hopes that all our plans would go smoothly.

As afternoon made its way to evening, we surrounded ourselves with an arsenal of hair spray, hair clips, curlers, curling iron, combs, and brushes. Mom and I began our transformation into a couple of sophisticated ladies.

"Let me help you," I offered to mom, helping her to fasten the curlers into her hair.

"Honey, now let me help you," and she returned the favor.

We spent the time in our beauty headquarters laughing and smiling, in our desperate attempts to pull off the looks we'd envisioned in our heads. But something was missing. As joyful an event as this was, it was tinged with sadness.

"Mom, I keep thinking something is missing, and I think I know what it is. It's Sandi."

"I know what I need," I said, and made my way over to my bedroom to find the locket Cliff and Sandi had given me for my sixteenth birthday

"Mom, can you help me put this on?"

"Sure. That's better." Mom smiled knowingly, her heart clearly feeling the absence as well.

We arrived at the hotel, and Cliff greeted us with corsages, boutonnieres, and a congratulatory banner for our parents.

We were a sharp looking family as we stood in the entrance, all dressed up and posing for Grace, as she took pictures of us.

Every member of our family who'd been able to make the trip to Edmonton was there. And as I glimpsed the looks of pure joy that crossed my parents' faces, I knew all the effort had been more than worth it.

As their song, *"Could I Have This Dance?"* played, and they made their way to the middle of the dance floor, I had a glimpse of the life they'd had as newlyweds. Their love seemed as fresh as it must have been on their wedding day forty years before. As children, we have few opportunities to thank our parents for all they do for us on a daily basis; the debt of gratitude I felt I owed them seemed impossible to repay. But here, at this moment, I felt I had made a dent in that debt.

Chapter Nineteen

The road to recovery seemed to be such a long one; I was still fighting my disease, the IBS, and my respiratory problems, but at least I had more control. Even though it might take me months to get back to where I was before I'd started, at least I felt like I was on the way. My weight was continuing to improve, and while food was still an issue for me, it wasn't controlling me. And once the iron supplementation started to kick in, it felt like I was waking up to the world again; the renewed energy made me feel like I was seeing things for the first time.

I was twenty-six years of age now, and I increasingly began to question myself.

"What am I going to do with the rest of my life?"

I wanted a career – but I needed a career I could negotiate despite my health issues. I knew also, that one of the biggest challenges I might face would be the perception of others with regards to my capabilities.

I went into the living room where Mom was sitting.

"Honey how are you today?"

"Mom, I woke up and thought, 'What am I going to do with my life?'"

"Oh, my – what a heavy thought so early in the day."

Thoughts of pursuing a career in writing were forefront in my mind; so we went to visit Reilly, a counselor at the college I had applied to before. Reilly escorted us into her office.

"I love to write," I told her. "Do you have any suggestions?"

"Well, there is the journalism program, but what kind of writing do you do?"

"I've been writing my memoir, but most importantly I'm working on a novel."

"There is a new program starting up as part of the Bachelor of Applied Communications in Professional Writing. It has a creative writing stream so you can explore both types of writing. You can enroll in the General Studies Program to get the necessary requirements, and by the end of the year you'll have a good idea whether you can manage – or even like – attending classes. What do you think?" she asked.

"I think that sounds great."

It would be quite a while before I'd be able to actually start the writing program, but it felt good to have a legitimate plan to lead me down the career path.

As the first day of class approached I met with Reilly and campus security to try and address any and all issues that might arise during my attendance. I'd have no aide at the college, so I yet again had to address that seemingly simple issue of using the washrooms – this tactical problem became a fashion issue as well. I needed pants with a belt loop that I could easily pull them up and down.

Any kind of stretch pants were out because they balled up and my fingers – at least the four I could use –lacked strength to untwist them. The arthritis in my fingers was essentially like having all my fingers taped tightly together and under; it meant that I approached every activity like you would if you were wearing mitts. Plus, my arms couldn't reach that far around my back to pull at the elastic. Then there was the challenge of grabbing the washroom's door handle, pulling it back, and driving in quickly enough so that it wouldn't close before I got in. To deal with transferring myself from the wheelchair to the toilet, I undertook a regiment of leg exercises to build up my strength.

I had thought I might want a locker at school, but the physical structure of the locker sets made that decision for me. The top row of lockers was too high for me to reach from a seated position, and the bottom rung too low for me to bend down. So I'd be hauling all my books and binders back and forth. Speaking of which, even the binder proved to be an issue. The silver rings that clasped shut to keep all those crisp, lined white pages in place were impossible for me to open myself, so I had to make sure that I had the pages inserted at home. God forbid if I needed to change their order during the day!

All this, and classes hadn't even started yet.

At six a.m. on the first day of class, I wiped the sleep from my eyes. Reality set in – this was no dress rehearsal; today I was a college student with a full course load. Something felt more *real* this time around, and I steeled my resolve that this time, no matter what, I was going to see this through.

The sun was peeking through the morning clouds, highlighting all the possibilities of the coming day. As I rode down the lift from our front porch into the semi-darkness, I closed my eyes and took one calming breath. The air was chilly, but it refreshed me and invigorated my spirit. Today I faced a full slate of classes; it was one of the days that posed the largest scheduling challenge. But I loved a good challenge. We pulled up to the college, and Dad stopped the car. I watched as dozens of cars unloaded their cargo of passengers. It was official; there was no going back.

I rolled through the electric doors of the college entrance and into the foyer. A throng of students rushed around me, trying desperately to figure out where their classrooms were located; at least I wasn't alone in that. I drove over to the elevator and pressed the button with my pencil – a trick I'd devised since I knew the buttons would be out of my reach. The second floor of building two was my destination. Two other students joined me.

The glass elevator provided a view of students and instructors rushing up and down the winding staircases. As I exited, I was met by a hallway lined with rows of lockers on one side, and a series of rooms along the other. The hallway was a noisy mesh of conversations.

Once inside my classroom, I found a place to sit. Unfortunately the multi-leveled seating structures hadn't offered me much choice – I had to sit smack-dab in the front, off to the side.

Wish I was invisible.

I looked around and saw a student with her head firmly on her desk, possibly asleep, while another looked brightly ahead of her, raring to go. In front of me was a desk where a pile of stacked books sat, soon to be joined by the grandmotherly-looking teacher.

"Hello," she said warmly as she saw me sitting by the table.

I drove over to her desk.

"Hello. My name is Alison. I have to leave class at about 8:55 so I can go take some medication. Is that going to be alright?"

"That will be just fine, Alison. Go right ahead and leave the classroom when it's time. Thanks for telling me."

"You're welcome." I headed back over to my spot. In a few minutes, the class bells rang, and it all began.

The first class was about introducing the students to the syllabus and the course requirements, a stark reminder that this was serious business. The expectations, essays, quizzes, and all the content I was responsible for in just this one class was mind-blowing.

What am I doing here in a classroom? What am I doing in college? I'm twenty-six years old. I'm kidding myself if I think I can do this.

The prof let us out early, which gave me time to use my inhaler in the washroom – somehow I felt as though I needed it more than ever. As I grabbed the heavy washroom door handle and pulled, my wheelchair got wedged in the way and I couldn't get the door to open all the way. Backing up would only render the door's handle impossible to reach. Finally, after maneuvering and finding a position that solved both challenges, I finally got myself lined up in the doorway for an approach. While the door did crash loudly into my wheelchair as it closed, I did manage to make it in there.

Success.

I felt like I'd reached the top of Mount Everest. It seemed like all this might be possible, after all.

My life became a blur of studying, reading, and deadlines. The fall term was half over, and the midterm exams were approaching at breakneck speed. Of all the assignments so far, my presentation with another student in my Play Analysis course was causing me the greatest amount of anxiety. We had to take a section of the play *Hamlet*, analyze it, and then present our findings in front of the entire class.

It may seem strange, given my love of performance, but public speaking has never been one of my favorite things. There's a kind of security when words are cloaked in rhythms and melodies. Without that musical structure, I feel naked.

Our instructor had had us pull our partners' names out of a hat; we chose our play excerpts similarly. Ironically, the section of the play I was assigned was one which the character sings a sad little song about her desperation and conflict.

In another stroke of coincidence, my partner was the only other differently-abled student in the class, a young deaf man. After a few meetings, and keeping in touch through e-mail, the assignment started to come together. On one occasion, my partner and I were talking about how much he loved music (with the assistance of his hearing aid).

"You could sing the part that the character does," he said to me. "If you could do that, I'm sure it would help our presentation mark. Would you sing?"

"Well ... I haven't sung in a long time, and my voice isn't in great shape."

"Try to sing. It would be more interesting to have someone singing. It would make us stand out from all the other regular old boring presentations."

"Alright – alright! I'll try, but no promises."

219

I'd already been fretting a bit about memorizing our scripts, and now there was the added stress of the song. I worked diligently visiting my vocal warm-ups, trying to get my voice back into shape. My voice and articulation not only had to be clear and concise, but also had to demonstrate the emotion of the character in that moment.

The two of us went up to the front of the classroom; my stomach was in my throat. As we started our presentation, the rows of students watching us seemed unending. The small singing selection was close to the end; so for the rest of our time *onstage*, I was distracted by the knowledge of its impending arrival. It would either work brilliantly to our advantage, or sink us. Page by page, we went through our script, taking turns to explain and discuss the meaning behind the scenes, as we understood them. And then the moment arrived.

I looked down at the carpeted floor; then slowly moved my eyes up over my feet, to the sheet of lyrics that sat on my lap.

Just do it.

I took a deep breath and began to sing. I mean, *really* sing. I sang like I hadn't in ages. And it was *Hamlet!* As I sang out, I peeked around the classroom just long enough to see the clock in the back of the room, to make sure we were hitting our presentation time.

My partner had been right; the song clinched it for us. Our marks were glowing, and later my instructor approached me.

"Alison, the students thought I'd had something to do with that song – I wish I had! The looks on their faces were priceless, you have a beautiful voice."

Searching for Normal
Alison Neuman

Receiving such a compliment from a real theatre aficionado meant a great deal to me, but there was no time to rest on my laurels! It was a delicate balance, juggling classes, assignments, life, social activities, and my health. But as my disease appeared to be in remission, it felt like it was completely doable.

The following day in psychology class, a volleyball player sat next to me, and we chatted before the prof arrived, about our plans.

"Tonight I have volleyball practice. Then we're moving, so I have to finish packing and still find time to read this chapter! What're you up to after class?"

"Tonight I'm going out with a friend for coffee, but then it's study time for me as well."

The moment I uttered those words, it struck me.

Wait. I've found my definition of normal. I'm normal.

The meaning I had been chasing for over twenty years; I was living it. Instead of feeling like a freak all the time, or like someone living in an entirely different world, I was one of *them*. Sitting there, in class, my eyes started to fill with tears, while I silently enjoyed my latest accomplishment.

The next day, during a meeting with my Play Analysis instructor, we discussed my revelation.

"Alison, why would you want to be normal like everyone else? You are special."

I hadn't been expecting that response, and his question stayed with me.

What does it really mean to be normal? Does being like everyone else mean being plain?

It took me some time to realize it, but he was right. I realized that I needed to embrace my difference, because that difference had made me the

221

person I am today. It had given me strength, compassion, understanding, and a lust for life I was not sure I would have had, had everything in my life been *normal*.

Perhaps what made me different did set me apart from the mainstream, but perhaps the mainstream was far too dependent on setting out labels and definitions and pressuring us all to fit into the confines of their perceived *normal*.

My difference is what makes my life interesting. I'd rather be anything but normal.

Chapter Twenty

While I'd stopped trying to mold my existence into someone else's conception of normality, I still struggled to determine what path I wanted my life to take. Getting into the PROW program would be a challenge, for sure, but I wouldn't entertain the notion that I wasn't a good enough writer. Having tackled a full course load successfully I felt certain that I could meet the difficult demands of the program. There was a three-hour entrance exam to assess our writing skills, however; that was more than a little daunting.

On the day of the examination, Dad took the day off work so he and Mom could take me to the college. Upon reaching the City Centre Campus, Mom and Dad wished me the best of luck and left me in my electric wheelchair to make my way to the examination room. My counselor had contacted the invigilator beforehand, and they'd agreed to give me time and a half to complete it; so I prepared myself for the possibility that I might find myself a prisoner in the room for four and a half hours. The pressure of knowing that my future plans rested on the outcome of this one test manifested itself in a tightness that spread throughout my arms and legs.

With the room number in hand, I set off into a previously undiscovered part of campus. As I drove up to the room, a young woman greeted me.

"Alison, I presume?" she said as she walked up to me.

223

"Yes. And I can have time and a half, correct?" I just wanted to give myself piece of mind that the arrangements had been made.

She looked down her nose and frowned.

"If absolutely necessary you can, but you should be able to finish it like everyone else. We need to see that you can complete the exercises the same as everyone else does. Follow me."

It was hardly the auspicious start I'd been hoping for. The woman's attitude had shaken me. It left me wondering if this program would be the right fit for me, after all.

I felt like I was starting the exam with already one strike against me.

The woman led me down a narrow hallway and into a room where two other women were waiting, seated around a large boardroom table. The room had few furnishings other than a clock; and the window looked out at one of the college's towers. We all introduced ourselves. I found that the two other women were writers who already had either business or publishing experience. Me, I was just tinkering around with a memoir and coming in with a love of the written word.

The PROW official brought in our exam booklets and scrap paper. She made a point of checking the clock at the top of the hour and telling us that our three hours began at that exact moment. I started by taking my first pencil and filling my name and details into the program booklet – a desperate attempt to stall and give myself a moment to calm down after my interaction with the monitor, and brush aside my concerns over my lack of writing experience relative to my fellow examinees.

Instead of previewing the entire exam I started immediately with the first assignment. Having been in a college-level English class and written a few essays, the first few questions caused me little to no stress. I would have liked to have availed myself of the scrap paper, if only to help me organize my thoughts, but writing and rewriting took too much effort for my hands. I would need to manage my energy to permit me to complete the marathon writing session that lay ahead.

I glanced up to gather my thoughts and found that the woman in the far corner was a few pages ahead of me in the booklet. The other woman's head was lowered, deep in thought. The clock signaled the passing of an hour with its loud ticking.

The next portion of the exam required us to write a book review. This would have been considerably less difficult to do had I actually had the time to read for pleasure in the last five years. The entirety of my reading time had been dedicated to text books and course requirements, so I was forced to utilize one of those sources for the review. I had to source from those same materials for the next section, where we were asked to write a blurb for the back of a book. Remembering the exact details of a textbook proved to be far more difficult than it would have been for a novel; but I'd dug my own hole on that one.

When I next consulted the clock, it revealed another hour of time had passed; I felt heartened to know that two hours, or more, remained for me should I require it. My hands were blackened from the lead of pencil shavings and eraser tailings.

Next was technical writing. We were provided with two possible scenarios to demonstrate our abilities in instructional writing: tying a shoe or wrapping package. For a moment I panicked; I hadn't tied a shoelace in eight years. I couldn't even reach my feet, let alone tie my shoes! So like it or not, *wrapping a package* was the only option available to me.

The final section was for definitions. The words ranged from easy, to hard, to ones I'd never even heard of. For the latter, my goal was just to break down the word's etymology the best I could, in order to express its meaning in my own words.

Once I'd finished the definitions I checked the clock once again and saw that I had finished with an hour and a half to spare, while the other two women were still scribbling away.

That can't be right. I must have missed something.

I frantically flipped back through the book, panicking that I'd missed a crucial, and time-consuming, section, but I hadn't. So with time to spare, I looked over the exam in the hopes that I might catch any errors in those last minutes. Satisfied with my product, I moved towards the exit. One of the women looked to have finished reviewing her test as well, and she whispered good luck to me as she exited the room. As she walked out, fresh hallway air rushed in and brought with it a sense of satisfaction, as I handed the booklet over to the invigilator, well before the allotted time had run out.

Now began the waiting game.

In a few weeks, a letter arrived in the mail from MacEwan. As Mom brought it over to me, my hopes began to fade quickly; it was a skinny envelope.

"I'm going to go bring the laundry up," Mom said, leaving me in privacy with the letter.

"If I'm crying you'll know I didn't get in."

I watched her go to the stairs and with a deep breath, opened he letter.

When Mom came back up the stairs and walked into the kitchen, her face sank when she saw my emotional state.

"Oh honey …"

"Mom, I was accepted." I went over to her and hugged her tight.

"Oh you! Your tears, I thought you ... Of course you were accepted."

It was a conditional acceptance, contingent on the completion of an additional English course, but the only words that mattered to me in that moment were those that had opened the letter: *"Congratulations."* The bottom line was that I had been accepted. Tears of joy ran down my face as I realized just how badly I'd wanted to be a part of this program.

As fall rolled around, I prepared myself as best I could for the demands of the new program. Up first would be required courses on rhetoric and grammar. However in the months since my acceptance, Dermy had made an unexpected visit, making life more difficult for me. I would need Mom to accompany me to my classes to act as my aide. Right from the start, Mom insisted she was to be introduced to others as Violet. She "didn't think having a Mommy-tag-along at college was cool." But in front of the other students, I proudly called her Mom.

By the time the first week of classes was over, I was filled with a looming dread that suffocated the excitement I'd initially felt at being well on my way to becoming a writer. The syllabi for the courses all indicated that an extremely high standard would be applied to our work. Both my grammar and rhetoric classes were taught by the same instructor, and she was tough. She deducted a standard five percent for each error in an essay, up to thirty percent. I'd always known that the strength of my writing had come from my ideas and characterization – not my grammar.

In the past, my grades for essay work had always been in the high eighties, so I hoped that maybe I could manage to scrape my way through. Not that scraping by was good enough; I wanted to retain my grade point average from the previous year. But life was intervening again. As much as I wanted to be successful in my coursework, I was finding it difficult to balance the demands of school with my need to spend more time with my mother.

I had seen how my Grandma K had struggled after her stroke, and it had made me very aware of the fact that cardiac issues tended to be genetic. Grandma K's stroke left her in the company of strangers as she no longer knew her family, or her best friend, her daughter, Vi. The thought of losing Mom, and not having her know who I was, reinforced a terror that drove me to keep a watchful eye out in an attempt to protect her.

In the last months I'd started to become increasingly concerned about Mom's health. I'd observed a marked difference in her behavior, of late. Mom would be extremely tired in the early evenings; and her memory was just not as sharp as it once was. She would forget small details like where items were in our house, or places and people from her past.

On my urging, we visited the doctor where they ordered a CT scan. It revealed that she did have a narrowing of her blood vessels, but her blood pressure wasn't high. The doctor thought that perhaps Mom had had a small stroke, but the test was inconclusive since they had no baseline to which they could compare the results.

Pre-emptively, I became cholesterol Nazi. I focused all my efforts around planning healthy meals and minimizing our intake of sweets. Mom also reduced the number of cigarettes she smoked – and those were only allowed outside of the house. We also went for walks more often, with her pushing me around the block or the mall if the weather was too inclement. I was determined to do whatever was necessary to keep her healthy. But I also vowed that each evening, I would make the effort to spend quality time with her. Even if she just wanted to watch TV or read, I would be there with her. I'd never taken our time together for granted, but I was going to make certain that I treasured it.

At school my grammar classes continued to be a struggle for me; every new assignment felt like an adventure in confusion. A quiz early on had revealed to my instructor that my parsing skills were not up to the high standards needed to succeed in the course. It was hard to not to get distracted at times by my aching body. I was being assaulted by so much information, and at such a fast pace, that at times I felt as though I was trying to bail from a sinking ship with a teaspoon. The results of my first essay attempt in Grammar and Rhetoric revealed that I still needed more practice and patience; so I sought out help from the campus student services.

After reworking the paper with their assistance – working diligently to weed out all my mistakes – I was utterly disheartened to find that when my paper was returned to me, the mark had not improved greatly. What was the point of working so hard if I wasn't going to be rewarded at all for those efforts?

It seemed pointless; regardless of the effort I invested in my assignments, the end result was the same. My health simply couldn't bear the stress from the courses; and I was starting to think that the ramifications of pushing myself so hard were going to be too much for my immune system to bear.

The day of the final exam, I sat alone at a large boardroom table as the clock ticked the minutes away. The laptop I'd been provided had its grammar and spell-check functions disengaged; I knew I was walking a tightrope. Despite my misgivings, I did my best, but I left feeling less than optimistic.

The marks were posted on my instructor's office door a few weeks later. As I drove into the department and down the long narrow hallway to his office, I felt a twinge of anxiety in my stomach. I scanned down the list of grades, searching for my ID number. The results ranged from very high, to complete failure; I hoped against hope that mine was not one of the latter. Finally, my eyes fell on my number. I scanned across the page to the corresponding grade, and there it was. There was the proof that all my hard work had been worth it. I'd been nearly frantic that this class would be the end of the line for me in the program. But now I knew that no matter what they threw at me, I would be able to handle it.

As I entered the second year of my Bachelor's of Applied Communications in Professional Writing program, I began to better understand the politics and business end of writing. Each day was a journey filled with winding puzzles of syntax and words, and the struggle to find my own voice and style. What made it all worthwhile to me, was the healing nature of the work. There is something therapeutic about spilling your soul onto that blank piece of white paper. Writing allowed me to go beyond the limitations of my body. But while the process of writing had always felt effortless and natural to me, navigating the coarse waters of grammar, formatting, and style had always limited the scope of my abilities –confining, rather than freeing, me.

I approached the first day of the new term, with the familiar feeling of anticipation and dread. My goal this year was to attend classes independently. When the morning arrived, I moved to my desk chair, only half-awake, and completed the stretches my physiotherapist had taught me, designed to keep my joints from becoming rigid and useless. I pulled my fingers closed and then forced them apart again so many times, I lost count. I pushed my reluctant legs and shoulders up and down. These were the exercises for the body – the paces my college classes would put me through in short time would keep my mind from becoming lazy.

"I will be out there in a minute. Need to check my face," I yelled down to my mom. I looked at myself in the large mirror and leaned in to try and focus my blurry reflection. I spread on pink lip gloss, dabbing off the extra with a tissue. Before, a professional or neat appearance hadn't particularly mattered to me, but now a neat appearance made me feel more confident.

"Need some help?" Mom asked.

"No thank you. I'll be right out."

Before we left the house I did that one final *out the door* check – nothing hanging from my nose? Check! Nothing sticking in-between my teeth – check! Lip gloss –check!

I felt like a small child – full, giddy with excitement on Christmas morning. Mom helped me slip on my black faux leather *rock star* jacket, and I went out the door. Dad and I slowly rode down the lift and were greeted by the sun splashing up over the horizon, belying the cool, crisp air.

Inside the warm car Mom, Dad, and I were all filled with positive energy.

"Are my snacks and medication in the bag, Mom?"

"Yes, I double-checked."

Dad drove us up the hill towards downtown, the college's tall clock tower peeking up from the horizon. After we parked, Dad unlinked my seatbelt and pulled my wheelchair out of the trunk. The green bike rack – the electronic doors – the windows – those familiar signposts triggered in me the same anxiety that had hit me this time last year. Suddenly, I felt as though I was weighted down. Nausea bubbled up in my throat, and I froze.

Take a deep breath. Swallow your anxiety.

I took a deep breath to regain my composure and transferred myself over into my manual wheelchair.

Mom wheeled me through the electronic doors and into the college.

I'm in!

We swerved through the long lines of students waiting to purchase their parking passes and arrived at the security office. The attendant recognized me.

"Alison, I've put a call in, so someone will bring your electric wheelchair 'round right away."

Students walked by talking and laughing, and the place was filled with that same buzz of excitement and energy; it was invigorating. My chair arrived, and my independence regained, I sped away on my own towards the classroom. The breeze as I zipped down the hallway left my hair tousled in its wake. Year two would definitely test my mettle in terms of my independence and, ultimately, my self-confidence. But after motoring down to the classroom, I was greeted by a bevy of familiar faces, all waiting for the classroom door to be opened. The college really felt like my second home now.

"Hey, Alison! How was your summer? How is your health?" a friend asked.

"Good. My health is still acting…" but as I went off into my brief explanation, my friend's eyes drifted away, and her body started to lean off towards the wall; I got the impression she'd asked simply to be polite.

"How was your summer?" I asked her instead. Her eyed darted back towards me, and she leaned closer to where I was seated.

"It was good, but passed by too quickly," she answered.

The prof arrived to open the door for us, and we both entered the classroom.

"Welcome back to classes. Did everyone have a good summer?" the instructor asked.

And from that moment I was back to the world of deadlines and daily challenges. The countdown to the finish line was on; only four months to go.

Chapter Twenty-One

Since beginning PROW, trying to schedule the required classes around the demands of my health had been a challenge. I was no longer able to attend evening classes due to an overwhelming exhaustion that set in during late afternoon. Bouts with anemia had stripped away much of my oxygen, often making it difficult to concentrate or learn new concepts. Because of that, I'd been reluctant to take some of the more demanding courses that were required of my program.

By mid-October I was dragging my body through each day. My immune system was affecting my concentration, making my brain sluggish and learning a trial. Adding to this, my body fought me on each endeavor to read. No matter in what position I held my head, reading inevitably caused me neck pain and headaches, and often a black spot would appear in my vision, covering the words in front of me. It forced me to take the simple task of reading a short paperback out over weeks.

November arrived, signaling the fact that just two months remained in the program. At that time we began studying *In Cold Blood* in one of my most useful classes, Creative Nonfiction. It had been invaluable to me for crafting dialogue, ensuring narrative flow, and the importance of *show, don't tell*. On one particular day, we were watching the film adaptation of the seminal book. The black and white movie flickered on a large screen at the front of the classroom, the soundtrack evoking a nostalgia that gave us another take on the book's mood. An hour into the movie the instructor brought in a tray filled with tubs of popcorn. I hadn't eaten popcorn since 1995 out of concern it might upset my sensitive system. But as the tall tubs were handed to the students, the room started to fill with that distinct aroma of the movie theatre. The sound of crunching was all around me and I was seriously tempted. A couple of days earlier, on my birthday, I'd had a piece of rich, but tasty, birthday cake without any ramifications. I figured that since it was a Friday, it wouldn't be a big deal if I paid the price for my temptation the next day.

So I picked up a piece, the popcorn slick with butter. I popped it carefully into my mouth and let the salty flavor dissolve onto my tongue. The sense memory it evoked took me to another place. I became so entranced with the sensations of eating, that I stopped watching the movie entirely. Time and again, my hand disappeared into the vat of greasy, salty popcorn. It felt like a perfect moment – sitting in that classroom, filling my face, watching a movie in a class I devoted to exploring my passions.

The bliss from that moment faded quickly in my next class, when we received news of our next assignment. We were required to write a thirty to fifty page manual to demonstrate our technical writing skills, adhering to rigorous structural and grammatical standards. Knowing how demanding this project would be, I set out to writing almost immediately. My plan was to create a manual designed to assist in finding one's way around the college. Two sets of instructions would be included: one set of instructions for physically disabled individuals, and one for able-bodied individuals. Thirty to forty blurry hours passed by as I wrote, planned, executed and edited. I spent hours each day staring at the brightly lit monitor, creating charts and layouts, and arguing fruitlessly with my computer programs. In the end, it looked quite professional – with its colorful graphics, colorful tabs, drawings, tables, and text.

The final product was something I was proud of, and I handed it in with a certain amount of excitement, tinged with apprehension. When they were handed back, I peeled back the cover of the manual slowly, and checked the mark.

Sixty-eight percent!

I was ready to quit writing.

My old nemesis had reared its ugly head – grammar. Grammar to a writer is like pitch to a singer. If you don't have it, you can't sing. If my grammar was so poor, should I even be writing?

I kept telling myself that there was plenty of time to improve. That something I was so passionate about had to be meant to be.

I kept telling myself this, but on a bad day, that wasn't so easy to remember.

On one of those days, I found myself out buying groceries with some friends, when an attack began. My neck began to throb, and over the course of the next few minutes it grew increasingly difficult for me to think. Soon, it was impossible for me to hold a conversation. I checked out almost robotically, painting a fake smile on my face so we could rush home as quickly as possible.

As we drove home I did my best to hide my concern from everyone. After all, on some of my worst days I had always managed to drag myself to class; I had become a master at disguising how I was really feeling. I never want to show my peers any weakness. When they would ask me how I was doing, I refused to tell them the truth. My conditioned responses were always just "good" or, "I'm hanging in there."

It was hard to explain to anyone else how these attacks left me feeling, and even more difficult to convey that it might be months to years before Dermy went into remission again. The last time my disease dropped in, the visit had lasted approximately ten years. And there was also the possibility that it might not go into remission, that my current health woes would be permanent. On a day like that, it wasn't a world of possibilities to me; it was a world full of hardship.

Mid-term, it was announced to us that our classes were going to be moved to a different campus on the west side of town. Not only was that campus not accessibility-friendly, it was a logistical nightmare for me to get to. What was a minor inconvenience for other students put my future in real jeopardy. My father simply wouldn't be able to drive me, and I never expected him to with his increasing age. While he was able to drive me in the mornings, in the evenings I would have to arrange to take DATS (the city's Disabled Adults Transit Service) to get me home.

As a result of the complex scheduling, each Thursday I was stuck at campus on my own for a three-hour break between classes. So after lunch I would sit in the library at a table near the compact disk library. It was there one day, as students rushed back and forth, that I had the idea for a novel – a secret agent in-training who just happened to be in a wheelchair. As the idea flourished in my mind, I found that that three-hour break was something I looked forward to. I would lose myself in Elissa's – my protagonist – world, and time flew by. Sitting in that library, *Ice Rose*, was born.

For my last year in the program, I had deliberately saved the two classes I was most looking forward to, until the end – Screenwriting, and Publishing Prose. The screen writing class was exciting, but I found all the formatting and rules a real challenge.

It was the prose class that filled me with anticipation, and the timing of the class was fortuitous in light of my work on *Ice* Rose. The class filled with students, I had gotten to know over the years, all of whom were all amazing writers. We would each write a chapter of a work, and then hand it in to be work-shopped by the rest of the group. Our instructor, Craig Gillespie, was an author who I very much admired. In fact, I'd taken the course largely to have an opportunity to work with him. I hoped that maybe some of his knowledge and skill would rub off on me.

As we all handed in our chapters for work-shopping, I grew increasingly anxious. I knew I would receive constructive criticism, but my issues with grammar always left me feeling inadequate and vulnerable. And as the critique began, it appeared this was evident in my writing.

"I want to love Elissa, but her feelings and experiences with her disability seem to be distanced from us. You need to tear down the wall and let us in … let us love her," one student said.

That sentiment was echoed by other students and the instructor, and I worked hard to keep those

Searching for Normal
Alison Neuman

comments in mind as I approached the next chapter. In order for Elissa to share what it was like to have a disability, I would actually have to let the readers in on how *I* experienced being disabled; I had to bare my soul. I felt naked revealing that part of myself; but that said, I knew they were right.

For the final part of our program, we were required to complete a practicum in the community – the idea being that we would garner experience writing in a professional capacity in a workplace setting. Given my latest writing project, and my previous writing experiences, we managed to set up a practicum with a hospital, where I'd been a patient several times before. I thought it the perfect opportunity to gain added insight for *Ice Rose* while completing my final credits for PROW.

Things had changed a bit since I'd last been there, recovering from surgery. I found that the cafeteria no longer served foods I could eat, and surprisingly, the washrooms on the main level where I would be working weren't accessible for me by wheelchair; nothing was ever simple. On my first day, I was introduced to Ted, a coordinator, who would be overseeing my practicum. My program required that a high percentage of my work with them involve writing. Yet despite knowing this, shortly after I arrived, Ted had me phoning volunteers for a lottery booth they were running.

"It'll be good for you to learn how to use the phone as telemarketers like to hire people like you."

I did a double-take.

He didn't actually just say what I think he said, did he? 'People like me'? Really?

239

I was pretty sure he didn't mean college-educated people by that. Rather, it was quite clear to me that from his perspective, the fact that I used a wheelchair to get around the world, meant I was a lesser human being. I was floored. This had come from someone who worked in rehabilitation, after all! I took a deep breath and tried to maintain composure.

"Now I'm going to call you so you can practice talking on the phone."

Nope, not adding insult to injury at all.

Rather than blowing up, I just did what he asked. I figured that I was better off simply blowing him away with my results. And I did.

Each time I booked a volunteer, the positive feedback rolled in; and Ted was forced to acknowledge how positively people responded to me. Yet he continued to treat me like a second-class citizen. A few weeks later he came into my tiny office and announced that he wanted me to introduce myself at a board meeting, and then promptly leave; it was clear I was being used as some token person with a disability.

A short while later, when my practicum instructor checked in with me, she became concerned by the lack of writing projects Ted was giving me. After what I imagine was a colorful discussion with Ted, I was soon writing significantly more. But despite finally getting to do what I'd been sent there to do, I wanted to get out of there as quickly as possible. It was a hostile environment, and I knew I was being manipulated. But I refused to quit and give Ted the satisfaction of thinking that I wasn't good enough to do the job.

One day when Ted was heading out, leaving me in the office, I stopped him.

"Can you please leave the office door open?" I asked him. "If there's a fire I can't open these doors."

"You're fine. If there's a fire they'll come around and check," Ted said as he closed the door before even letting me respond.

But with the door closed, not only was I concerned about my safety, but neither could I get out to use the washroom, let alone get back in. Well, about middle-way through my shift the fire alarm went off and all I could do was sit back and hope I was safe. I couldn't see any smoke out the window, but I was sure I could smell it. Soon the alarm shut off and an *all clear* was announced over the intercom. But there had been a fire. In fact, it had been just across the hall from the office where I had been sitting. But of course, I'd been the one made to feel silly asking them to keep the door open.

The last day of work couldn't have come soon enough. Shockingly, Ted actually had the gall to ask me to take on additional hours after my practicum was over. He'd belittled me, and been nothing but patronizing and rude. As if to cap off my tenure there perfectly, he condescendingly kissed me on the forehead. I didn't think I'd ever been happier to leave a chapter of my life behind.

With the completion of my practicum, my course requirements also came to an end. Our graduation was held at the Winspear Centre, an incredible venue where I'd seen several concerts. Cliff, Dad, and Mom were all firmly planted in my cheering section. My counselor met me to lead me to a box close to the stage where she could wheel me up to accept my diploma.

I was swimming in my blue robe, but Dad had given me a lovely corsage to accent it, and I was thrilled to be able to mark the accomplishment with my fellow writers. As I crossed the stage, I could hear Grace and Zinnia in the audience cheering me as well. Even if it wasn't for a performance, I reveled in being on that stage – the accomplishment was no less monumental in my books.

Chapter Twenty-Two

The fall made its presence known as cold winds began to seep into both my and mother's joints, causing arthritis flair-ups for the both of us. I had been doing whatever I could to safeguard my mother's health, but despite my best efforts, we were hit with a devastating blow. As if out of nowhere, suddenly Mom had trouble speaking and could no longer recognize Dad. The caregiver in me kicked into high gear; after feeding her a little soup and getting her cleaned and dressed, we piled into Cliff's car to the doctor's office. He scheduled another CT, and an appointment with a specialist.

As I sat with her, it felt like my best friend was gone. Her body sat next to me, but her recent memories, the very things that preserved our closeness, were gone. It seemed likely to all of us that she'd had a stroke – the very thing that had so terrified me. Everything I'd done and I still couldn't protect her!

I prayed for a miracle. I knew there could never be enough time together, but still I wanted more. I felt selfish, but I felt like there was no way I could manage the world without her. The thought of coping with all the challenges she'd guided me through without her absolutely terrified me.

How am I supposed to do this alone?

We were sent to the rehabilitation hospital so that Mom could see a specialist in geriatrics. She was taken in by herself for tests while we filled in various questionnaires. While our GP also assumed she'd had a stroke, he needed a specialist's opinion on how to proceed.

As we filled out the various forms, detailing her health history, I could not help but feel a sense of guilt settle into my bones. How could this have happened? One doctor had suggested that smoking had likely been a strong contributing factor, and I wished I'd been stricter with her about it. I'd gone outside with Mom when she used to have her cigarettes, thinking at least I was monitoring how many she had. But deep down, I wondered if I'd been too complacent about it.

When the results came back, the specialist determined that she'd developed dementia – the result of three small strokes. He prescribed some medication to assist her in her recovery, but it was clear that serious damage had been done.

I wanted to prepare myself for the worst, and I didn't want them to sugar-coat it,

"How long does she have?" I asked the specialist.

"It could be around seven years, but everyone is different."

Seven years.

I was somewhat heartened – seven years seemed like an eternity. But when I got back home, my internet search of dementia quickly reduced me to tears. Each prognosis had the sufferer's identity slowly stripped away, until their spirit, their essence completely disappeared. There was no cure; there was no way to stop it. For the first time in my life, I truly felt alone.

Medications helped Mom in her rehabilitation from the strokes, and we began to be able to reopen the lines of communication as her vocabulary returned. But I had resigned myself to the fact that things would by and large get worse, and not better. And I'd also resigned myself to the fact that as her condition progressed, and she ultimately passed away, much of my life would come to an end. There was no way that I could manage in this big scary world without her. She made the world feel safe. She made life livable when my disease stole everything else from me.

"There will be some new meds, they'll help..." Cliff tried to reassure me.

I clung to that small hope as much as I could; I so wanted anything to give her back all the pieces of her life that were being stolen away. I gladly became her caregiver, helping her with all the daily tasks of living as she had done for me for so many years. I took over her dressing, bathing, and cooking as much as I could. And as the disease progressed, I became adept at playing the sort of charades necessary to interpret the meaning of the words that were lost to her as they traveled through the neurons of her brain. It seemed particularly cruel to me, in my endeavor to become a writer, that language was letting her down.

But the world kept turning as we waited for an appointment with the specialist to put in place a treatment plan, and we tried to make life as *normal* as possible for Mom as we could. Every Friday night, Uncle Ingmar and Cliff would come for supper. I planned and cooked the meals prior, and Mom would always help. Each time she did, her efforts were tinged with sadness, when she'd enter the kitchen.

"I saw this young girl," she'd say, "who needed help. I want to help."

A couple of weeks after we'd been given new medications, it felt like we'd been granted that miracle. Mom was back to where she had been before the

245

stroke. It was as though the last few weeks had just been a bad dream. She was back to doing everything around the house she had done before; she was back to being *Mom*. I knew that this might not be permanent, but I was grateful for however much time the medication might grant us. It gave me the opportunity to say everything I wanted, so that I'd never have regrets.

"Mom, I love you. I am sorry for everything I ever said that might have hurt you."

"Oh honey, I love you too. Me, too – but it's all okay, don't worry," she said.

During the weeks of mom's illness, I'd abandoned my writing; there was little question that I needed to. But as her condition improved, I realized that on top of caring for mom, I needed to write to be happy, to maintain my sanity. So in the spring, when a local company was looking for contractors, I applied. I must have done something right during my interview, because they hired me. I was able to complete the work from home, allowing me to continue to spend time with Mom. It was a short-term contract though, and while it gave me the confidence to know that I could make a living at technical writing, it was clear that my heart wasn't really in it. Creative writing was what fueled me. If recent events had taught me anything, it was that life was too short, so I turned my writing attention back to *Ice Rose.* Ever since I'd completed the program I'd been itching to get published, and Elissa's story was how I was going to do it.

It began a couple of days after Dad's birthday. First I thought it was the flu, but the pain and fatigue was so reluctant to leave my body, I knew there must be something else going on. After several weeks of being unable to function, my family and friends finally coaxed me into going to see Dr. Respect.

"I know you never wanted to be on it, Alison," he said, "but could we try Prednisone for a few weeks?"

Prednisone. A steroid. Precisely the class of drugs that I'd had to spend months in hospital getting weaned off of. But the amount of pain I was in, and how quickly my body seemed to be getting out of control, left me with little choice, and I consented.

Within a few weeks my body was moving, and the pain had lessened. But my blood tests revealed inflammation, and confirmed for certain that I was not dealing with the flu, but with another bout of Dermy. Knowing that, Dr. Respect began to reduce the Prednisone and started me on weekly Methotrexate pills. Methotrexate is a serious med that is used in larger doses as chemotherapy to treat some types of cancer. Dr. Respect also talked me into getting the ball rolling to see a surgeon for my joint pain.

The side effects of the Methotrexate could be brutal. After a dose of the pills that had left me unable to eat or even move – each time I tried to focus my thoughts I felt like I'd been hit in the head with a brick – they prescribed the medication in injection form. I always felt somewhat nervous getting the injections though – the stuff was so powerful that if even a drop or two got on my clothes, that item would have to be thrown out, for fear it might contaminate my family's clothing. The pills gave me terrible headaches for two days; but the pain and burning throughout my body began to abate, and I hoped that we might be able to knock Dermy out for the count.

After one of my doctor's visits, I was resting on my bed while Mom was rubbing the anti-inflammatory gel on my knee. We were watching music videos on the television.

"I sure wish I could have a record out," I said.

"Why don't you?"

"Well, I have a couple of songs that were co-written. But costs a lot and..."

Mom stopped me,

"If it's something you want to do, then you should do it."

And of course, she was right – we knew that better than anyone.

With that, my journey to having a single produced began. One of the women I'd met during a singing competition had composed some music to lyrics I had written some time ago. Unfortunately she had since moved, and I couldn't consult her anymore. I had two songs ready to go, but a typical single had three. I scoured the internet and eventually found a songwriter out of the Maritimes to work with. In just a few weeks I had an amazing backing track in my hands.

Despite their side effects, the medications had given me enough control over my body to open up my lungs to hit high notes; so when I felt confident enough, Grace and I headed to the studio. It was the same studio I'd visited on a tour as a teen. It seemed surreal to be back there recording, rather than just visiting and goofing off.

I struggled to keep my nerves from getting the best of me; it had been four years since I'd sung in public. The engineer showed me into the studio and placed a table and mic in front of me. Mom sat beside me for moral support.

"Alright, I've turned the table and mic away from the booth so you don't have to look at me. That should help your nerves. Let's try each song twice, and we'll use the best take." Mom smiled and quietly watched me recording. It felt like it went by in the blink of an eye.

Several weeks later, a box of 100 shrink-wrapped compact disks arrived at the studio. The engineer pulled one out of the box and presented it to me. My face hurt, I was smiling so wide. There it was – my CD, and the fulfillment of a fourteen-year-old girl's dream.

I gave copies to my family and friends, but never released it generally. While their responses to the songs were overwhelmingly positive, you always think you can do things a little bit better – and who knows, maybe I would improve it some day. But for now, having it in my hands was all that mattered.

Yet another childhood dream soon reared its head again. One day as I was sifting through a series of email forwards, I hit one in particular that not only shocked, but inspired me, and awakened a part of my soul that had lain dormant for well over twenty years. Attached to the email was a link to a video of two dancers who had won a dance competition. That in itself was no big deal. But what floored me was the fact that one of the dancers had a mobility aid. Instantly, I was brought back to a time in my childhood where I had visions of being a dancer. It was a dream I had shelved when I'd come to rely on a wheelchair for movement. But there it was, right in front of me – a vision that rekindled that passion within me.

It had never occurred to me that I could still pursue dancing with my condition. The rules of the dance world had always seemed too rigid to have room for my arthritic, misshaped limbs or my wheelchair. But after seeing this video, I began eagerly scouring the internet for dance groups that had differently-abled members. I contacted a local dance studio for information, and they put me in touch with iDANCE, Edmonton Integrated Dance, a group that held classes at the rehabilitation hospital. Classes had started just a few weeks prior, but given its location, I was fearful that the instruction would be more clinical or therapeutically-based than artistic.

Despite my skepticism, I decided to at least give it a try. Cliff drove me down to the center, and we made our way to the quiet atrium where a group of individuals had gathered amongst the bookshelves, tables and chairs. For a brief moment I thought about going home. Every single person in this room was a stranger. Several were in wheelchairs, one was using a walker, and the rest were walking. A woman with pink highlights in her hair introduced herself to me as Lillian, and beckoned me over. She was positively oozing joy.

"Come in and join us," she said as she went towards the front of the room.

Cliff pushed me towards the centre of the room, but I kept myself back a bit closer to the door, in case I needed to make a hasty exit.

The room was filled with smiles and an almost palpable joy. A woman with beautiful curly black hair glided over to where Cliff and I had relocated. Her small frame was able to make her wheelchair glide with such incredible elegance. She introduced herself as Isabel.

"Welcome to iDANCE. Feel free to take any part of the dance for your own," she said, as she returned to the front of the room to help Lillian set up her stereo.

"I'm not a dancer. I'll be in the TV lounge, and you have your cell," Cliff said as he waited for my permission to send him out to freedom. As he walked to the door, another dancer introduced herself to me as Harmony. She glided about in her wheelchair, full of grace. Next was Celyn, who moved about fluidly in her electric wheelchair, followed by Kerri, Kate, and Aiden – each of whom enthusiastically invited me to join in.

Each of their movements embodied the spirit and rhythm of the music so beautifully. But I kept to the back of the room where I was safe to explore the movement while hiding my own discomfort. As we began to move around the space I was very quickly reminded of how my disability, even in a room of people with disabilities, still made me stand out. While all the manual wheelchair users pushed themselves around smoothly, I awkwardly tried to pull my heavy wheelchair around. I soon became fatigued and was stuck in one spot. As I looked around the room each of the wheelchair dancers were doing the choreography with all the art and craft of the standing, and walking, dancers.

But while I was intimidated by the grace and skill of the dancers around me, by the end of the class I knew this was an environment I would thrive in. I soon was attending every possible class, ultimately coming to enjoy the challenges and physicality involved in trying to get my body to move in a manner that mirrored the other dancers, while retaining my uniqueness. Lillian and Isabel, two senior dancers, provided me with instruction on how to take the choreography and make it body-specific, and allow each of us to blossom as a dancer. I wasn't someone in a wheelchair trying to dance. I was a dancer.

Chapter Twenty-Three

I dreaded my appointment with the surgeon; I'd been stubbornly avoiding surgery for years. Cliff came with me on the drive to the other end of the city and waited with me until the surgeon came in. Dr. Freedom was well-built, and much younger than myself. He began by going over what he'd observed in my X-rays, and then went over all the possible negative outcomes of the surgery. He could tell I was wary of it all.

"You're brave. When you're ready, let us know. Until then let's try a cortisone injection."

Adding to my wariness, was the fact that everything in the rest of my life seemed to be falling back into place, and I wasn't eager to change that. Mom had been doing extremely well, and I'd received notice from a publisher that they were interested in my work. In fact, not only did they request to see the rest of *Ice Rose,* but a contract followed its receipt! In the meantime, I was finding such a lot of joy in my weekly dance classes. We were working towards our class recital – yet another performance opportunity I'd once thought unlikely to occur.

The morning of my first hip cortisone injection, I thought I would be sick. Mom had once had such an injection; and she had found it both painful and unable to provide her with any relief. The idea of going through all that and not feeling any better didn't thrill me, but if it kept surgery at bay, then I would do it. Cliff drove me to the doctor's office, and we were soon waiting in the lobby. Finally I was directed to the changing room before being sent for X-rays. We were then led to a room with a tall table situated beneath a massive X-ray machine hanging overhead. Cliff helped me up on the table, before leaving when the technician who would perform the injection arrived. He was an older man with a British accent. He walked me through the entire process of draping, freezing and the injection itself. In fact, he even let me watch. As the freezing coursed through me, it felt like a large elastic band was being slapped against my skin – but no worse than a Novocain shot at the dentist. Ten minutes later, I was back in the car, and we were on our way home. Having the hip frozen felt wonderful; just a few weeks later, and the intensity of the pain I'd been feeling had become nothing more than a memory.

Finally able to concentrate on my work again, I began the laborious editing process for *Ice Rose*. We worked to ensure consistency throughout the manuscript, and sought out any grammatical errors that might be hiding inside. I didn't want anything that might threaten to take the reader out of the world I'd created, for even a second. If my name was going to be on it, I wanted to make sure it was a quality product.

The release date for *Ice Rose: A Young Adult Spy Novel* was set for September 18, 2010. It was just a few months away and still so much work was left to do –choosing the book cover, getting an author photo taken and then, of course, planning a launch. As I started to think about the event, I realized that I wanted to be able to use the opportunity to thank the Rainbow Society for all they had done for me and my family. So

I came up with the idea of holding an auction as part of the event, as well as donating proceeds from each book sold to the organization. It felt only right that since my publishing dreams had come true, I use the opportunity to raise funds to have a child's dreams come true as well.

I made arrangements with the Rainbow Society and made reservations at a local fondue restaurant for the fundraiser/launch then began the challenge of collecting items for the charity auction. Over the next several weeks I sent out hundreds of emails and made phone calls to every contact I knew. The donations began to pour in: Justine Bieber tickets, hot air balloon rides, segway tours, the list went on. Most vitally, the final round of editing had been completed, and *Ice Rose* was on its way to the printer.

We were in the final throes of preparing for the release event when the first shipment arrived at our doorstep. It took all the willpower I had not to rip the box open. Finally, Cliff yelled at me.

"Get out there right now, and open your books."

I slit open the box, my hands almost shaking from excitement. I lifted off a layer of paper to reveal a stack of books with my name emblazoned on them. There are no words to describe the sense of accomplishment I felt at that moment; it's a feeling I'll treasure forever. The girl, who for her whole life had struggled to be *ordinary*, had done something extraordinary that countless others can only dream of.

The night of the launch several relatives arrived from out of town to help ensure that the things went off without a hitch, including my cousin Bailey and her husband, Gabriel. A fellow author would act as MC, and Grace's niece, Rae-lyn, was going to do a reading. I entered the restaurant to find my helpers had already been busy rushing around, transforming the restaurant into a den where secret agents would meet – in fitting with the book's theme. They'd also set up a sales area with the books, a donation box, and all the auction items had been set out, awaiting their opening bids.

Before I knew it, the festivities had begun, and Craig was making his opening remarks. This was the man who had acted as my mentor, who had been instrumental in helping me achieve my dream; and here he was, extolling my virtues to a rapt audience. When the moment came for me to speak, I looked out at all the friends and family who filled the room, and was overwhelmed by the occasion. I abandoned the speech cards I had carefully written out, and decided to speak from the heart.

Out of the corner of my eye I glimpsed my mother smiling, with tears in her eyes. We had done it. She had always believed in me. And through all the rejections I'd faced – both with the book and in life – It was her conviction that had kept me going. I was beyond grateful for the fact that she was fully present on that night – grateful she was able to share in that moment with me completely; it wouldn't have been right without her.

After the speeches wrapped up, I moved to the autograph area, and soon there was a line-up stretching out of the banquet room and around in the main restaurant. Thousands of dollars in sales rolled in, and with much of it going directly to the Rainbow Society I hoped that my contribution would help another child's fantasy be actualized.

With the launch firmly in the rear-view mirror, I was able to return my attention to my dance activities. Each day I attended a class acted as an awakening for my spirit. As the recital date approached, I would watch other dancers as they rehearsed and often found myself in tears. Yes, there were bodies of massively different shapes, sizes, and abilities. But each one of them performed the choreography with such elegance and artistry. It was dance, plain and simple – with all the inherent beauty that comes from movement that is filled with passion. Isabel, in particular, held my attention. Her wheelchair was a part of her, and her movement seemed so effortless. She was exactly the kind of dancer I hoped to be one day.

Soon the recital day arrived, and I found myself waiting in the wings with my iDANCE teeshirt. Mom, Dad and Cliff were all in the audience, waiting for my entrance. Backstage a group was filming a documentary on dance and interviewed each of us. I struggled to maintain my composure and answer the questions as articulately as I could – but admittedly, I was nervous.

Shortly before we were due to start, Lillian approached me, "We're having Orchesis auditions soon. The rehearsals run from September to January. We would really like you to join us and be a part of it."

It had come from out of nowhere,

"Can I think about it and let you know?"

Orchesis was a modern dance group on the university campus, and the prospect of working with them was a little intimidating.

"Sure. I'll send you the information, and when rehearsals are, and you can let me know," she said.

As she walked away, Kerri approached me.

"You have to join us. We already have a part in mind for you!"

I was beyond flattered to have been asked, but I had to put it all on the shelf for the moment; there were so many things I'd have to consider before giving them an answer.

Moments later we were on stage and dancing. No matter how my hip and knee were aching and hurting the rest of the time, in the instants where I was dancing, there was no pain in my body – only joy. For just a few minutes I felt as though I was in control of my body. Despite all my body's plans to sabotage me, I had made it through. Dermy had not been able to take dance away from me.

Chapter Twenty-Four

The recital had been a success, and after much consideration I decided to take Lillian and Kerri up on their offer to join Orchesis as part of iDANCE. The first rehearsal was at the University of Alberta, so Cliff drove me over in the evening. He pulled into a parking spot near a basketball court.

"I brought my laptop," he told me, "so I'm just going to wait in here and do some work."

"You sure? You can come inside. It's safer," I said. I wasn't thrilled with him staying in the dark parking lot alone in the cold.

"Don't you worry. If I get cold I'll come in. If you need me call."

We got out of the warmth and safety of the car, and Cliff pushed me the few feet to the entrance of the building. My body shook and shivered in the cool air, despite my winter attire. We passed the students working out on the elliptical equipment of the gym and lifting weights, and made our way over to the elevator. As the doors opened we were greeted by a warm breeze and the scent of chlorine, indicating that a pool must be in the vicinity. While my lungs indicated their displeasure making me cough a bit, they adapted fairly quickly.

Relief swept over me when I entered the hallway and saw Isabel, Lillian and many others from iDANCE. Cliff parked me in the group before leaving me in the safety of my fellow dancers. As we sat in the hallway, we all aired our concerns with one another. More than a few of us were *'freaked out'* and excited. As the previous dance class began to exit the studio we were allowed to enter the room. The room was a real dance studio. A huge grin spread across my face as I saw the bars along the windowed wall, the floor to ceiling wall mirrors, and the hardwood floors. It was my first time in a professional dance space, and I took it all in.

As we began to warm up, my legs felt especially weak. My body seemed reluctant to allow me to pull myself across the medium-sized room. We began some partner work, and it quickly became apparent to me that something wasn't quite right. As the other dancers moved past me, their movements began to leave something like a tail of light behind them. I made it through the rehearsal, but promptly went to bed after we got home.

I was starting to feel like I just couldn't hack it. A week or so prior, what should have been an exciting event was marred by pain and fatigue. I'd had my first official book signing as a real author. The morning of the event I'd noticed a great deal of pain on one of my butt cheeks, but I was determined to go through with it. Cliff stayed with me by my little table near the front door, as I spoke to customers coming in. I developed a sort of *perma-grin*, going robotically through the motions, trying to hide how much my body was aching. Part of me was excited to be there, but part of me was screaming to go home and crawl into bed. After a while, even my vision started to blur, and it dawned on me that there was likely a calcification ready to erupt. I knew I had little recourse but to head back to the doctor.

Trying to build a life of my own seemed to be more and more challenging. As the relationship with my mother continued to change, I couldn't help but feel empty and lonely at times. Now I felt like I was less able to manage—even with just my own care. Basic daily tasks felt either overwhelming or impossible. It was at that time that I began to switch my focus to looking for a man who could, at least, restore some of the security I felt I was losing. But the limits of my mode of transportation, and my general social isolation, made meeting men a challenge. Or at least, it made the pool of men to choose from much smaller that I would have liked – after all, you can only have the cable man, gas meter reader and mailman visit so often. So in an effort to meet someone new, I tried to go out more often.

One such event, however, did little to bolster my enthusiasm for jumping into the dating fray. A female acquaintance and I began a discussion on dating, and she decided to share with me her accumulated *wisdom*. She was telling me that as we age, the number of men attracted to older women diminishes. She then suggested that my *prospects* were even worse.

"My male acquaintances would sadly have nothing to do with you—because of your wheelchair," she said without a hint of embarrassment. "It will be a challenge to find a man who will."

I sat there in near shock that she was saying this not only to me, but in front of any of the other people milling around and chatting. Still, it affected me, and I felt a kind of sinking feeling in the pit of my stomach.

"You should lower your standards a bit," she kept going, "maybe look for a much older man, someone with children."

It got worse.

"Go on a blind date and don't mention your wheelchair in advance, just show up, and once they get to meet you, maybe they'll accept your wheelchair."

Ever since I was a child I had dreamed of being a girlfriend, a wife, a mother, and here she basically saying I should give it up and just settle for whatever dregs the world had left for me. She was making it sound as though love, for me, was pretty much about shopping in the *as is* section of a department store.

I walked away feeling like a piece of furniture that didn't make the cut due to a defect. I should just stick a proverbial *"bargain"* sticker on my forehead, and hope for someone who was desperate. It struck me that maybe she should re-evaluate the type of people she was spending her time with, but I kept silent.

While my relationships to date hadn't been as lengthy as I would have liked, I knew I deserved more than the kind of objectification she was meting out to me – and I certainly knew that the types of men with whom she was keeping company were not the types I'd ever be interested in spending time with. My wheelchair is a small part of me which affects neither my brain, my heart, nor my ability to love. What I need is a man who can see that, and for that man, I can wait. I can learn to be strong and independent.

A few days later I went to Dr. Respect's office for an appointment. As he examined the area where I'd felt the calcification, I could see the concern on his face.

"It looks like there's an infection there," he said placing a thermometer under my tongue.

He wrote out a prescription before telling me the words I'd been dreading.

"Maybe we need to admit you to the hospital for IV antibiotics."

My heart sank. I couldn't leave Mom.

"Could we try some compounds? I know it's not perfect, but I really can't leave Mom on her own."

"I don't like the way that rash is traveling, and you've got a fever. We'll give the compounds a shot, but you have to promise me that if it's not working in a few days that you'll go to the hospital for outpatient IVs. Deal?"

"Deal."

The drugstore assured us that they'd be able to make a version of the scrip to accommodate my allergies. But when Cliff returned with the medications, we discovered that they weren't allergen free. I was furious, and since it was after dinner, we'd have to go to emergency to get my medications. It took a five hour wait before I was finally led into an examination room.

It was past eleven, my temperature was over a hundred, and I was exhausted. When the doctor came into the room he did little to relax my already frayed nerves.

"We are going to open that up and drain it," he announced.

"Can't you give me some antibiotics instead?" I asked.

This wasn't what my doctor had recommended, and I was a bit stunned that he was taking this unorthodox approach.

"It needs to be cleaned out. Then I'll give you a dose of meds – it'll lessen the pain."

I knew in my gut that this wasn't a good idea. Every doctor I'd ever had, had agreed that opening up the calcifications was not a good idea. But I didn't have the energy to fight, and of course, the doctor was supposed to know best!

A little after twelve the doctor, accompanied by a resident and nurse returned. I'd still gotten no pain meds, my fever was continuing to climb, and now he was jabbing me with needles full of local anesthetic. Each shot felt like he was shoving a jagged knife into my body. My ears began to ring and the room to spin. Through the haze I heard the doctor joking with the resident.

"I'm surprised she didn't pass out," he said to which the resident laughed. I was beyond angry at the fact that my suffering was an amusement to them.

"She's strong," the nurse interjected.

The doctor opened and drained the area.

"Look at the stuff coming out. There was more in there than I thought. Send some to the lab for analysis – I don't think this is all puss."

It's calcium, you idiot.

"I've packed it up. You might want to wait a couple of days, and then take out the packing. It'll hurt," he laughed. "Stay off of it for a few days. Get her a crushed antibiotic and she can leave."

And he left. It had been years since I'd been so objectified by a doctor, and especially one who seemed to have no clue what he was dealing with.

I rushed out of that hospital with Cliff in an effort to get as much distance between the doctor and me.

As we pulled away from the hospital, I told Cliff what had happened in the exam room.

"Alison, why didn't you tell me? I would have done something!"

"I guess I was just in shock. I thought he'd get better."

"Tomorrow you call your specialist."

It was two-thirty in the morning before I was in bed. My butt was packed so full of dressing that there was a raised area I couldn't sit on. As the freezing wore off; the pressure was certainly less, but I was still in pain and feverish.

When I spoke with Dr. Respect the next day, he confirmed my fears; it shouldn't have been opened up, and he'd given me the wrong antibiotics. This time we had no choice but to go in for IV treatment. The entire experience had shaken my faith in doctors in a way I hadn't experienced for over a decade.

Each day I would sit in the outpatient infusion center and read my book, waiting for the IV to give me the power to fight off the infection. By the end of the week, I had become nearly non-existent. I dreaded each dressing change – each time the tweezers pressed the cotton material into the deep crevices of the wound it felt like tiny shards of glass were being packed in.

The following week I managed to make it back to dance class, with a warning to Lillian that I'd have to take things slow. I was still struggling to keep my thoughts clear, and it took extra effort to imprint the choreography in my memory. January was approaching quickly, and so too was the production of *Orchesis Dance Motif*. Before I knew it, tech week had arrived. From Sunday to Saturday we would have to be at the theatre for rehearsals and lighting and blocking.

"That week is going to kill you," a fellow dancer had warned me. This was not precisely what I wanted to hear, given that the week would also see me getting my regular cortisone injections. After each injection, joint mobility was always limited for a few days; I knew this would be a challenge during a week where I'd be dancing daily.

The performances were being held at the Myer Horowitz, and the hectic pace of the schedule became clear almost immediately. But, although there was an element of fear involved in all of the preparations, I was more exhilarated than anything else. I was being given the opportunity to perform in a professional show, with all the lights, staging, and costumes that that entailed. As I entered the lobby I was struck by the fact that despite all the varying heights and body types, I was the sole dancer with a visible disability. But rather than feeling awkward, I felt tremendously honored that they felt iDANCE worthy of representation in their production.

Once in the theatre, we made our way down the ramp to a hallway leading to the stage, for the first lighting rehearsal. As we held our positions while they sorted out sound and lighting cues, the dancers chatted quietly back and forth. It seemed that everyone had a smile plastered on their face. Despite the tediousness of the task, it was hard not to revel in the fact that we would soon be performing to a live audience.

As we pulled up to the parking lot on dress rehearsal, I began to see one of the foreboding auras appear in my line of vision. I quickly took my medication in the hopes that I could stave off an on-coming migraine, but let Lillian know what was going on.

"If you need anything, if you need to go to the washroom to throw up, let me know, and I'll help you."

I hoped it wouldn't come to that.

I sat there, my head pounding, stomach churning. When a videographer approached me, I struggled to find my words. I was determined not to leave until the rehearsal was over. But onstage, when I reached over to Lillian in a choreographed move, my spacing was off, and I felt my balance slip. I managed to stop myself before falling completely out of my chair and on top of her. Lillian insisted that I skip the notes, and go home immediately after the rehearsal, despite my protestations. I did my best to rest that night, in the hopes that I'd be ready for the next day's performance.

I awoke the next day feeling pain in all my joints from the stress I'd put on my muscles the day before. While I wanted to absorb and enjoy the time leading up to Showtime, I felt as though there was a gloom hovering over me. The incident the day before had demonstrated a vulnerability to the choreographers I'd not wanted to show, and I feared that they might seek to limit my involvement in the future. Isabel and Lillian's words on the drive over to the venue are ones I will never forget.

"There will always be a place for you and your ability in iDANCE," Lillian said.

"Even if all you can do is move your eyes," Isabel added.

Walking into the dressing rooms I marveled at how gorgeous the dancers looked in their costumes. I

changed into the black yoga pants and fitted green shirt
I'd been assigned; it was a little tight for my liking, and
I needed some help to get it on, but we managed it. I
settled in at the counter in front of a tall mirror lined
with light bulbs just like in the movies, and started
working on my makeup. I was one of the lucky few
who was given some assistance on that front, since not
only was I new to stage makeup, but my limited
mobility made it difficult for me to manage on my
own.

Before I knew it, it was time for curtain rise, and I
waited backstage for our number to come up. Soon I
heard our cue, and Isabel, Kerri, and I took our places
on the darkened stage. The lights went up, the music
started, and I was in the zone. There was no pain and
no worries – I   was lost in the movement and the
moment. When I climbed back into my bed after the
next night's show, I felt so proud of what we'd all
accomplished, and that I'd done it in the company of
such beautiful dancers.

Having wrapped up the performance, I refocused
my attentions on my writing work. I was regularly
being asked to participate in local writing events and
give presentations both on my work, and on my
method. Offers to participate in school visits had been
extended to me, and I was honored to take them up on
it. It was an aspect of authorship I hadn't really
considered before, but one I quickly grew fond of. The
children at the visits were remarkably insightful, and
their level of enthusiasm, infectious.

I was also receiving recognition from my peers;
the Strathcona Writers Conference invited me to
present a workshop on characterization, an invite I

readily accepted. Of course, in familiar fashion, the morning of my *Building Better Characters* workshop, I woke to a migraine aura and had to dose up on meds and avoid eating. But while my body was drained, I was filled with a certain amount of adrenaline at the prospect of my first formal presentation to fellow writers. The adrenaline carried me through a successful workshop, leading to other opportunities to give back to all the communities that had supported me along the road to authorship.

In particular, Lillian and I began to ruminate about an idea for a children's camp based around the spy school premise in *Ice Rose*: Camp Mission Access. The idea behind the camp was two-fold: to inspire children between eight and twelve to engage with literature and embrace the arts; and, most importantly, encourage inclusiveness in our communities. As the season for school visits came to a close (mercifully since I was finding myself exhausted from the schedule), we began to plot out the design for the program. It would include four missions the kids would complete, each with an accompanying workshop: Mission Unidentified (writing and imagination), Mission Covert Skills (individual and teamwork challenges), Mission Stealth Moves (dance and movement), and Mission Entry (mystery solving).

One of the things that had always struck me during my camp experiences as a child, was that despite how well-meaning they were, the idea of having a *special* camp for children with disabilities had never sat well with me.

It was just another way that we were made to feel as though we were being *othered*; segregating us from so-called normal camps was just another way of telling us we didn't fit in. I always felt that important opportunities to teach children about diversity were being missed. So Camp Mission Access would have, as part of its mandate, children from all backgrounds, regardless of ability, income, ethnicity, or any other defining characteristics.

It seemed like fate then, when the Rainbow Society contacted me about speaking at an anniversary celebration they were planning. Here was an organization that worked to provide kids with the same feelings of inclusion I was hoping to achieve with the camp; I couldn't have asked for a more perfect reminder of how important the project was.

The event was held at the Space and Science Centre, and when Cliff and I showed up we were immediately greeted by a host of familiar faces. Speaker after speaker recounted the impact of having their wish granted had on their life. For many, like myself, it had had a profound and long-lasting impact on their lives – inspiring them to create new goals and dreams to bring to fruition. I spoke from my heart about the beach at Catalina, the sand wending its way between my toes, and more importantly, about how important the memories of that time were to me now; despite the fact that the dementia was slowly eroding her memories, Mom and I still spoke of that week. The evening proved to be the perfect way to keep me energized while dealing with the logistics of getting the camp rolling.

Officials at the rehabilitation hospital provided us with a room for the event, access to the ball pit, mats, obstacle equipment, flashlights, hula hoops and all the toys and physio equipment in the back room. I was lucky to also have access to an occupational therapist and a teacher to consult with about the activities and make sure they were age and disability appropriate. The days leading up to the camp were hectic though, and compounded by a nation-wide pain medication shortage. With absolutely no warning, the manufacturers had simply stopped production of vital medications, leaving many of us stranded. My medical team was finally able to find an adequate replacement, but it had made the long days of planning taxing.

But despite the hardships leading up to the launch of Camp Mission Access, it was exciting to see the project realized. I had hired a few members of iDANCE to participate as camp counselors along with the other professionals. The participants seemed to be incredibly eager, and they embraced the secret agent aspect of the camp with great gusto. But at the end of the day, the true measure of our success was reflected by the joy reflected on the faces of each of the *agents*, and the fact that not a single child had felt isolated or been made to feel as though they were lesser than any other.

Chapter Twenty-Five

As part of the requirement for getting a total hip replacement, I was required to attend a *teaching day* where I would be trained all the *dos and don'ts* of post-surgical life. The day started off with X-rays and a weigh-in (I was thrilled to find my weight was up to 99 pounds), and then proceed to viewing info-videos on the procedure with my fellow surgical candidates. As I watched them describe the process of cutting out and removing the joint, I started to feel like I could feel it in my very bones. And I felt alone. It would be the first surgery where Mom would not be at my side when I awoke.

I met with the various therapists afterwards, who outlined my rehabilitation exercises, and a nurse who reminded me that if a sore I had on my leg didn't heal in time, they'd have to cancel the procedure. I closed out the day with a consult with the anesthesiologist, who searched my spine to find an appropriate place to administer the anesthesia. To my surprise, and disappointment, he was recommending spinal, rather than general, sedation; this would minimize the risks of muscle damage. As if the whole idea of surgery was not scary enough, now I had to contend with a new, potentially traumatizing, element to it all – I'd actually be awake with a breathing tube shoved down my throat. I'd also been advised that because of my condition, my recovery would likely take place in an ICU – rather than in a regular ward with other

272

replacement patients – so I could be closely monitored for any complications.

It was becoming harder and harder to remember what the benefits of all this were supposed to be.

I tried my best to focus on other things as we continued the waiting game for a surgical date – namely on the upcoming performance. But as we began learning the choreography, I was struck by the fact that there was a strong possibility that I might not be able to participate. My reservations about this grew as the only other wheelchair was forced to drop out due to health reasons, which meant that either the piece might be cut entirely, or that I might have to replace her; neither option was appealing. At our next rehearsal, we discussed the piece as a group.

"Do you think the section should be taken out?" Lillian asked.

The consensus was almost immediate that we shouldn't, but the piece was designed specifically to include a wheelchair dancer, and no one felt comfortable with the idea of having a physically able dancer use a chair – it defeated the purpose. And that's when Lillian suggested that I do it.

I gulped, and raised my eyebrows.

"I can't. I can't replace her, she's too good – she's more advanced than me."

But the group felt strongly that I could do it, and once they made clear to me that they'd arrange the piece to work with my abilities, I began to warm to the idea. And after our first run-through for my new part I surprised myself at how much I was able to do.

I approached the performance of the piece at a local dance lab, with confidence and enthusiasm. But

273

as I sat in the audience watching the previous group perform, a black spot began to appear in my vision, and I felt my energy draining from me like the air escaping from a balloon. I gathered my quickly dwindling energy with a deep breath, and resolved to put on my best *character* to help get me through the piece.

My unsteadiness quickly materialized on stage as I found myself unsure of steps that just moments before I'd had emblazoned in my memory. My wheelchair became interlocked with another dancer's, creating a sharp scraping noise as we tried to break free. Then a newer section's choreography simply disappeared from my mind; and as I looked to my fellow performers for a reminder, they where completely blocked by the dark spot in my vision.

But despite the screw-ups (which thankfully weren't noticed by the audience), I gathered my composure for the finale of the piece, which required me to pop a giant balloon. It seemed the perfect action to express the frustration I'd been feeling – not only during the performance, but in all the months leading up to this moment. And when the time came, I did it with relish. And I nailed it!

Shortly after the close of the dance season, I received my surgery date. In less than a month, I would be making my way to the hospital and then to rehabilitation. I spent the week leading up to it cooking and freezing meals, in case they weren't able to provide me with food my system could tolerate. I'd tried to keep all the preparations as low-key as possible, as Mom's dementia was steadily worsening, and her ability to retain information and grasp more complex concepts became more hampered with each passing day.

She knew something was going on, and made a disturbing statement to me one day.

"I don't want the man to take you away," she said.

I reassured her I would always come back, but it broke my heart to leave her or to have her not fully comprehend what the reason was for my absence..

On the day of my surgery I was up at 5:30 a.m. for the home care attendant to help me shower. Cliff arrived to settle himself in for his stay at the house, and I finished packing my toiletries. When the time came to leave, I avoided an extended series of goodbyes.

"I love you, Mom. You be good now." Despite my best efforts, tears started to roll down my cheeks, and I rushed to leave the house. As much as I wanted to give Dad a better goodbye, he understood. Three weeks was an eternity in Mom's world, these days – and who could know what I might come home to.

"Sorry I'm a little emotional," I said to Cliff as he helped me transfer into the car.

"You don't trust me with Mom. Thanks!" he said, laughing.

"I'm a girl, we get emotional. Besides this is a long time away from Mom," I said, but I knew he understood.

En route we talked about the weather, music, whatever minute details we could think of to keep my mind off what would happen in the coming hours. Once I was checked in, we were sent up to a room where four other patients were being prepped for surgery. Some were in reclining chairs and some in beds; I was lucky to be given a bed. A nurse helped me with the sanitization process and getting changed. I climbed into the bed and she placed a heating blanket on me to help keep me warm.

After a respiratory technician came in to collect blood, Cliff told me that the ICU had a bed available for me post-surgery, which meant they would not have to postpone the surgery. While I was glad to hear it, I can't say I was thrilled by the fact that it meant that surgery would happen today, come hell or high water.

As I lay in the bed, patients came and went like an assembly line.

"You nervous?" Cliff asked.

I nodded.

"Don't be. Look – it's a well-oiled machine. Think how many surgeries they do each day, flawlessly."

He was right, but until I got that spinal, and they had me sedated, I knew there was no relaxation to be had. When they finally came for me, Cliff walked with us to the elevator before heading down the stairwell and back home. As I waited in an area where patients were having breathing tubes inserted, and listened to one patient half-screaming, I wanted so badly for the surgery to be over.

My anesthesiologist arrived.

"Alison can we try giving you this spinal without sedation? I'm concerned that sedating you might be hard on your lungs."

I didn't relish the thought, but I agreed and was moved to the prepping rooms. A flurry of professionals surrounded me before Dr. Freedom came over to my bedside.

"Okay Alison, let's try to get that hip fixed for you."

The anesthesiologist searched my spine for what felt like forever before starting the spinal injection. I lay on my side in a body vice as I waited for it to take effect. Finally the meds kicked in and tightness around my side abated. They strategically placed a blue sheet over my face to hide my view of the procedure. I waited, hearing the sound of drills, imagining that at any moment I would feel the slicing of skin and bones. But there was no pain to be had, and a kind resident stood near my head observing and chatting with me to keep me distracted. It was all going smoothly until the hour and a half mark my stomach began to churn, and I threw up. They administered some anti-nausea meds to help calm my stomach, and then the most heavenly words were uttered.

"Prep the next patient. She's done."

They transferred me to the ICU and on to a bed that felt like a cloud. Two nurses rushed to get me settled and wiped off my hip area.

"Good, she's awake – we'll have someone to talk to!" one of them said.

This room was tiny with just a small movable table at the end of the bed where a nurse could stay in order to monitor my vitals. My lungs were fine, and I felt pain-free. Of course, the spinal hadn't worn off yet.

"Cliff is on the phone, and wonders if you feel up to a visit?" the nurse said.

"Yes, please."

As I waited for him to come, I rested and watched some television. Cliff arrived with a People magazine so I could do the crossword puzzle. Our visit was short since the spinal was wearing off, and the discomfort was becoming intense. Once they were able to manage my pain they transferred me to a bed in a regular ward.

There were two other patients in my room, one of whom kept talking on her cell phone most of the night.

It made me yearn for the quiet and calm back in the ICU, and sleep was more elusive than I would have liked that night. I awoke to breakfast being brought in the next morning. I was so nervous not to unduly injure my new hip that I struggled to sit up at all. Later on, Dr. Freedom came in to update me on the surgery.

"When we got in there, your bones were like pudding; it was worse than I'd expected. I know it might be difficult with your schedule, but do you think it's possible to avoid weight-bearing for six weeks? It would give you time to heal."

"I think so, but will it affect my length of stay at the rehabilitation hospital?"

"It shouldn't," he answered.

As he left, I noted to myself that I felt remarkably good. But that evening when the nurses did their rounds they found that I had a fever, and my blood pressure had dropped. They started me on some meds, but my pressure just wouldn't normalize, and they announced that I'd have to have a blood transfusion. I wanted so badly to sleep. I lay watching the blood trickle down an intravenous tube and into my body, and eventually the mesmerizing drips allowed me to fade off into slumber.

My scheduled three days of hospitalization had turned into five, and at the end of that last day I was excited to be moving on to the next phase of my recovery.

Chapter Twenty-Six

I very nearly didn't make it to the rehabilitation center after my discharge from the hospital, as they were balking on having a non-weight-bearing patient. But Dr. Freedom had given them a stern talking-to, and finally the transfer arrangements were complete. Cliff came to the hospital to help me get packed, and take the overflow bags the ambulance didn't have room for.

The bright-faced and tattooed EMT introduced himself to me as he helped move me over to the stretcher. While chatting, we got on to the topic of my book, and he shouted to his partner.

"We have a famous author for our transfer today! She wrote a book, *Ice Rose*."

Secured in the back, I soaked in the view from the window and watched the traffic, sky, and buildings roll by. They unloaded me by the front entrance, and I got a taste of the warm sun on my pale skin. Once admitted, we traveled up to the ward where I would spend the next few weeks.

My roommate was an 81-year-old, also recovering from a hip replacement. She was a lovely woman, who introduced herself then made sure the nurse brought me some fresh ice water.

Cliff soon arrived and helped to get me settled, before going home to Mom and Dad. In an odd twist of fate, my dear friend Zinnia was also at the rehabilitation center, having herself been in a coma. The fact that I could just sit and hang out with a friend was beyond comforting, to both of us. It gave me the battery charge I needed to face the tasks that lay ahead.

The next day I met with my physiotherapist. While she'd likely come in with her own plan of attack, I knew she was in for a shock; my body played by its own rules. She spent the first forty-five minutes alone, just trying to figure out how to adapt the walker to accommodate my limited arm reach.

"That should make it more comfortable for you," she said, "Let's get you standing up and see how far you can hop."

Hopping? That wasn't a word that had entered my vocabulary in many years. Just imagining bringing the full force of my body to the ground brought waves of fear roaring throughout my very core. I simply didn't trust my new, fragile body. As I held on to the walker and pulled myself up, I had horrible visions of my joint slipping out of place. But I had to trust her, and carefully did a little hop. My right leg hit the floor and jolted my body, but my left hip absorbed the impact surprisingly well. I managed to go two meters, before my knee began to fail me, and weakness spread throughout my sore arms.

On the comfort of the mat the therapist worked on my knees to get them to straighten out. My right knee was not only permanently bent, but also was forcing my foot to the side. She measured my joints and all their various angles to measure my progress as well as insure that we didn't push ourselves beyond our physical limits. I was pleasantly surprised to find that after physio my body felt extremely relaxed.

A nutritionist was doing her best to help balance my meals, but I inevitably had to rely on my own stash of meals to keep me going. Despite my relatively bland lunch and supper fare, I looked forward to mealtime, as it was an opportunity to socialize with other patients, and with Zinnia. In an odd way, our daily routine felt almost spa-like. Granted, it was a pretty harsh spa that forced you to do a ridiculous amount of exercise. But still, I began to enjoy the routine; it helped me focus on my healing, something that was especially hard being away from my family.

A week or so in, I asked the staff about how long they expected my stay would be.

"Well, usually the patient, when they're not weight-bearing, stays until they are."

My heart sank as several other people on my care team confirmed this. It wouldn't be the three weeks we'd initially planned, not even close. When I pressed them for a discharge date, they told me October 17th. It would be nearly 10 weeks before I got home, and I started to panic. I felt like I was betraying my mother by being there for so long.

Grace tried to console me on one of her visits.

"It's your time. Take the time you need to heal."

I knew this was true, but I was my mother's primary caregiver, and I felt useless not being there. The following day during my visit with Cliff, we talked about it.

"I'll figure it out," he said to me. "I can maybe get extra respite care to come in while I go to work. We'll manage it."

And I knew Cliff would.

Soon I learned to sit up in bed unaided, which allowed me to be more independent. To ease my separation anxiety, my medical team advised me I could visit home during evenings and weekends. But by and large, I was exhausted each evening, and just getting to home was a major event; we had to hire a special van to transport me to and from home.

But on the way home that first time, I finally felt like I could breathe.

Dad greeted me by the front entry, and when I reached up, he wrapped me up in a big hug.

"Momma, look who's here! It's Alison," Dad said, and Mom made her way over to me from the couch.

For a moment my heart dropped as I wondered if she might not remember who I was.

"Hi honey, how are you?" she said, smiling and leading me over to the table. We sat for hours together –laughing, talking, playing music. We were a family again.

"This is the happiest I have seen mom in weeks," Cliff said to me, and my heart soared.

I worked hard to keep our schedule on track and avoid any further delays. Both the pain in my hip and the cracking I'd experienced prior to surgery had disappeared; each day I grew stronger, physically and mentally. With my new-found confidence, my OT was able to help me re-learn how to transfer myself into a car. We went down into the underground parking area of the hospital, and over to a silver Chevy Impala.

First she demonstrated how to swing on the seat and use her arms to lower herself on the seat. However the fact that she could use the full length of her arm, and I couldn't, might be a problem. She sensed my unease.

"Why don't we give it a try, and we can troubleshoot it as we go?"

I balanced on my right leg and, using my walker, hopped over to the car door. With both legs up against the car, I pivoted and placed my right arm against the side of the vehicle. Then I slowly leaned back, taking care to protect my hip. With my bottom resting on the seat, I used my arms to slide back into it. By this point only my feet were extended a tiny bit outside of the car.

"Now pull your legs into the car, but be careful not to twist," she instructed.

I did exactly that and, voilà! I was in the car. No more trying to fit my travel plans around booking the special vans. One of the puzzle pieces of my life had found its way back into place.

"Woohoo!" I shouted.

She laughed.

"I didn't realize it was such a big thing for you!"

We tried it one more time, and it went even more smoothly than the first; we both did a little dance to celebrate.

One of the things that made the iDANCE program so interesting, was that it allowed each participant to take dance choreography and adapt it to their individual ability. But as I started planning my return to iDANCE, I felt like I had lost much of the ability that I had before. I couldn't bend as easily, and it was difficult to push myself around in my chair. I also couldn't have another dancer sit in my lap.

I still wanted to dance, but the fear of breaking my hip was renewed each time I moved, and felt that twinge of discomfort move down my leg. After watching a rehearsal one day, Lillian walked me back to my room.

"I'm not sure I can ever be able to bend like I used to, and I don't want to take someone else's spot in Orchesis"

"If you want to be a part of Orchesis, we can make it happen."

"But I don't want to be a burden."

"I understand that you don't want to be a burden," she said. "I'd feel the same way. But this is our mandate. If you're not able to be in an entire number, then we'll get you in at the end – whatever we have to do."

Between physio and occupational therapy, I was learning what the safe range of movements was for my upper body. My left leg was still quite weak, but I worked to improve it. At my first returning iDANCE class, I held a bag on my lap to remind me to be careful.

All the community dancers welcomed me back, and I felt like I was at home again. Then Lillian started the warm-up exercises as I stretched and tried to figure out the best way to adapt to the new parameters of my body. My abilities had changed dramatically since the first time I'd stepped into that room, but it didn't matter. I had embraced the changes, and replaced all my fears with euphoria as I found my place, once again, amongst the other dancers.

Chapter Twenty-Seven

Zinnia had made so much progress in her own recovery that she was being discharged and was going home. While I was thrilled about it, I knew how much I'd miss her. I'd had a short visit home with my family for the long Thanksgiving weekend, and an evening with them afterwards to help tide me over, but I was anxious to get back to life as usual. Finally the day of my assessment with the specialist came. It was an early appointment, so I was up at 5:30 a.m. to get ready, before the healthcare aide Cliff had arranged to pick me up, arrived.

We had to stop first for X-rays, before making our way over to the hip and knee clinic. We checked in, and I sat in the exact same row, and same seats in the waiting room we had only a few months prior, before my surgery. So much had changed since then. Finally we were led into an exam room, and Dr. Freedom joined us a few minutes later.

"The bone looks perfect," Dr. Freedom said, beaming.

"Oh, that's wonderful!" My relief was palpable.

"So you can start putting weight down, but try and be careful for the six weeks. The muscles still need more time to heal. Any questions?"

"Do you think it would be safe for me to dance in my wheelchair, or should I wait until the three months are up?"

He smiled.

"In your wheelchair ... go for it."

Dr. Freedom left, and the physiotherapist came in to discuss my exercise plan for the coming weeks.

"Alison, now you can move on to the phase two exercises at the rehabilitation center. Start working on them, and I'd like to see you again in December."

Adrenaline pumped through my body as I reveled in the fact that I'd finally be able to put some weight on the joint; I'd be one step closer to getting my life back. I texted Cliff the good news, and made my way back.

My rehabilitation hospital physiotherapist stood in the doorway of my room, and walked over to me.

"So, what's the verdict?"

"I can bear weight," I said as I broke out my *excited arm* choreography.

I parked my wheelchair, and we prepared to move to phase two of my exercise regime – standing with both legs.

"Put less weight on your left leg at first," she instructed.

This tiny step had so many hopes and plans hinging on it. My muscles burned in a desperate attempt to dissuade me from walking. They'd spent a lot of weeks on vacation, and were reluctant to get back to work.

"So are you going to want to have an early discharge date?" she asked me, as I stood.

My answer surprised me.

"Can I let you know tomorrow?"

Yesterday I would have jumped at the possibility. But the amount of energy that just standing had required me to exert, was a stark reminder of how hard things were going to be when I got home. I needed to be able to take care of myself once I got home, and I couldn't let my over-eagerness cloud my judgment.

"Sounds good," she said.

I walked half the distance to the nurse's desk and started to run out of steam. But I kept pushing. That weekend, when I had gone home for Thanksgiving, I was reminded just why I was doing all this hard work.

I'd found Mom standing in the kitchen, and turned to her to ask, "Mom, can I have a hug?"

That, in my mind, was going to make the battle to stand all worth while. She opened up her arms to me; and as I stood there, she gave me the biggest hug I'd had in a very long time. Moments like that made it even more difficult to leave her again.

But the departures would be coming to an end, as my discharge date was now imminent. I had been in the hospital for fifty days and my body was stronger, but I was tired. At my final physio session, we parked by the double exercise bars as I readied myself to take some steps without my walker.

"I have to say, I'm nervous about you walking without your walker," she told me.

"Well too late, I'm leaving tomorrow!" I grinned.

"But I'm concerned that your hip isn't stretched out enough, you don't have as much bounce and give as other people."

"What can I do to reassure you?" I asked, knowing she only had my best interests at heart.

"Well, let's try and get you walking a little more 'pretty,'" she said as she pulled up a full-length mirror.

"Okay, now walk sideways and come back."

My left knee was grinding with each step, and my shoulders slumped.

"It just feels like it's never going to end," I said.

"What do you mean?"

"My knee started grinding a couple days ago."

She put her hands on my left knee and squatted down, as I stood so she could examine it.

"You know you'll eventually need surgery on them," my disappointment reflected in her eyes.

I sat, and she stretched my knees out to ease the pain.

"You know it won't get better, but you have to keep going," she said. "Are you ready to try the stairs?"

"Sure," I said.

She beckoned another therapist over.

"Come here, you have to see this."

Then she turned to me.

"Go ahead."

I began to work my way up the stairs, and to my surprise both my legs had the strength to hold me. It was the boost I needed. They weren't as strong as they could be, but at least they weren't getting worse. As the therapists cheered me on, I felt like it was another victory won.

After I finished packing up my remaining items, I sat down and took it all in.

I'm going home.

As a porter wheeled me and my walker down for my final physiotherapy meeting, I felt almost nostalgic. I was actually going to miss the visits with my therapists and trying to eke out a little bit more mobility from my body each day; the therapists were my every-day cheerleaders. I was going to miss my entire medical team, and the patients who had become my extended family.

288

When I reached the physio room, my therapist approached me,

"You don't need this anymore," she said, as she took the walker and moved it out of my way. "Okay, we're going to do a timed walking test. You need to go as fast as you can for ten meters."

There were pieces of colored tape on the floor that marked the start and finish lines. As I stood at the start I took a deep breath and focused. It was important to go quickly, but safely; and in a straight line.

Who did not love a good challenge?

She signaled the start of the stopwatch, and with all my might, I pushed off. At the halfway mark she glanced at the time.

"Wow."

At the finish line I took a second to rest, and then headed back to my chair.

"Twenty-two seconds – that's great! That's the equivalent of a two-lane highway, and you crossed it in time to get across during a light change."

"Really?" I asked, feeling excited.

"Yes."

I tried to convey to her my appreciation, but I still feel that mere words could not convey the depth of my gratitude for everything she'd done. She was the main reason I would be able to literally, walk out of this building.

"My one to two o'clock slot will not be the same."

"You'll get another awesome patient."

"But maybe not as challenging," she said, laughing.

Cliff met me when I returned to my room, and after a quick scan to make sure I'd packed everything, we made our way to the parking lot where, just a few weeks earlier, I had practiced transferring into a car. I climbed into Cliff's car, and we drove out into the bright natural light. My ears still hummed with the sounds of the hospital that would soon be all but forgotten. My body was pumped with hope and excitement for the future.

As we entered the house, Dad greeted me.

"I made your favorite chicken stuffing."

The hallway was filled with the delicious aroma of chicken and stuffing, and the sound of cartoons coming from the TV; I knew that I was home again.

But I had no time to rest on my laurels. I'd had a lot more downtime at the hospital, and really set my own schedule. The next day would start at 6 a.m. though, and I needed to prepare myself for the dramatic change in routine.

In the morning, I got up determined to make breakfast. In my head, I'd envisioned myself speeding around the kitchen, but the reality was quite different. By the time I'd delivered the food to the table, I was exhausted.

"If it's too much to make breakfast, I can help," Cliff told me. "It's really not a big deal."

"No, I can manage," I said. My pain levels were only about a four out of ten, and I could handle that.

Cliff left for work around 10:30, and I readied myself for the day. I was already exhausted, but I didn't let on to anyone.

As the day wore on, Mom struggled the more tired she became. As her weariness grew, her ability to complete simple tasks deteriorated, the culmination of which was evident at supper time. She was using her hands to eat, and while all Cliff and I cared about was that she eats independently, Dad had no patience for it.

"No, Momma! Use your fork!"

I tried to feed her, or show her how to use her spoon, but the results were the same.

"No, Momma, now look. It's all over the floor. I can't keep cleaning!"

By now she was in tears, and was trying so desperately to meet his expectations. He covered his head and rubbed his face. My patience was wearing thin, and without thinking, I lashed out.

"Dad, she doesn't understand! You're making me wish I hadn't come home!"

I knew I shouldn't have said it, but in that moment that was my truth. I had forgotten, that I while I was gone, they had been dealing with this on their own. They had been watching her get worse each day, and how difficult it must have been on him to watch the progression.

That evening Cliff turned to me and explained.

"It was really hard," he said, "the first two weeks with you in the hospital – really stressful. But then I realized that things are okay. Mom is okay, and I can do this. We all just have to be patient."

The next day calm had been restored in the house. Dad's outburst seemed to have helped stem the tide of anxiety he'd been feeling, and he was back to his joking self. We began to start settling back into a pattern, and I felt confident going to a dance class.

I was excited to see all the other dancers when I arrived, but I felt fragile and weak. My body was stiff and sore during the warm-up; instead of participating, I ended up watching, so I could conserve some energy for the choreography.

"I have a good part for you in our dance piece already," Lillian said to me.

When they started arm choreography I was ready to try. With my arms up and palms facing front, I brought them down to the sides, then out to the left and right. We practiced our poses and Lillian paired me up with Kate to work on finding a safe position that would also look interesting.

Lillian stopped us all and announced.

"Everyone this is good to know. Alison has to be careful as there are certain positions and angles she can't do anymore. We have to be very careful, so she does not over-extend and dislocate her hip. Alison, you let us know what you're comfortable with."

Then we worked together on an introduction that had another dancer and I traveling across the gym.

"I don't want Alison pushing herself," Lillian said, looking for a volunteer

Sophie and Kate both raced each other to try to push me first. They teased each other, and their joking made me feel less like a burden and more like a team member once more.

Back at home our evening was spent enjoying each other's company settling in to our evening routine. I fell asleep to the comforting sounds that I'd grown to miss so much, an odd calm having washed over me. It wasn't going to be easy – I knew that. But I was reminded about the parting wisdom shared to me by one of my fellow patients:

"Your life is enabled by imagination."

It would all just be about finding *my* new normal.

Epilogue

Mom's dementia has good days and bad days. Dementia is an affliction of change. Just when you think you've adapted to it, without mercy, it digs in its heels and alters your world once again. I see her frustration grow as each day it steals away another portion of life as she knew it.

She retains every ounce of her independence, and still has so much joy and love to share with all of us. We treasure every '*I love you*' and each hug, each moment, and each day. I tell her each day how proud I am of her, and how much I love her.

We work together as a team, with Dad doing as much cleaning and cooking as his aging body and emphysema will allow, and Cliff helping by providing support whenever and wherever he can.

As a family, we do not measure our success through wealth or fame. That goes double for me. My family has been pillars of strength that have formed the foundation of whom I am today. Being able to return the favor to them now, is my greatest achievement.

Other Select Books Published by Fireside Publications

Also written by Alison Neuman

Ice Rose: A Young Adult Spy Novel

The Crystal Angel	Olivia Claire High
Rose Cottage and	Olivia Claire High
Dreams: Shadows of the Night	Olivia Claire High
A Stranger's Eyes	Olivia Claire High

Essays: On Living with Alzheimer's Disease:	
The First Twelve Months	Lois Wilmoth-Bennett
The Furax Connection	Stephen L. Kanne
The Find	James J. Valko
Above Honor: Rachel's Story	Donald Himelstein
Beyond Forever	Taylor Shaye
The Cleansing	B.F. Eller
The Long Night Moon	Elizabeth Towles
18 Days in September	Allen N.Hunt, Ph.D
Independence Day Plague	Carla Lee Suson
Odds & Ends ~Bits & Pieces	Joye O'Keefe
The Serpent Sea	Linda Lehmann Masek
Where Danger Lurks	Judith Groudine Finkel
Texas Justice	Judith Groudine Finkel
Raven April	Nelson Trout
Amanda's Voice	Eileen Bennett
Silver Strands	Eileen Bennett

Made in the USA
Charleston, SC
30 October 2013